EMOTIONS EXPLAINED WITH BUFF DUDES

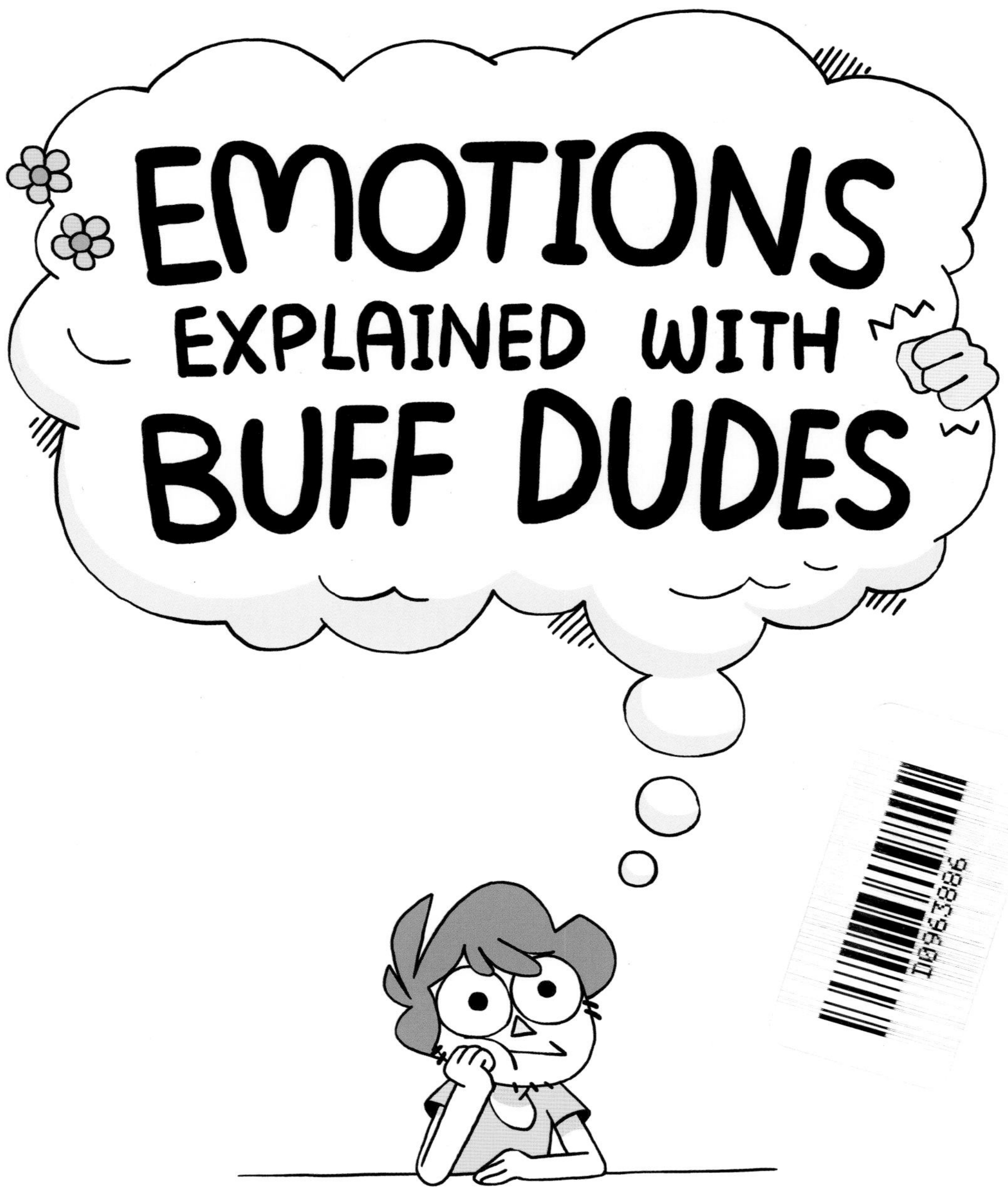

DEDICATED TO
MY DAD, ALEX,
MY MOM, YELENA,
AND MY GRANDMOTHER, NINA.

AND TO MY WONDERFUL READERS... ◡

EMOTIONS
EXPLAINED WITH
BUFF DUDES

OWLTURD
COMIX

ANDREW TSYASTON

Andrews McMeel
PUBLISHING®

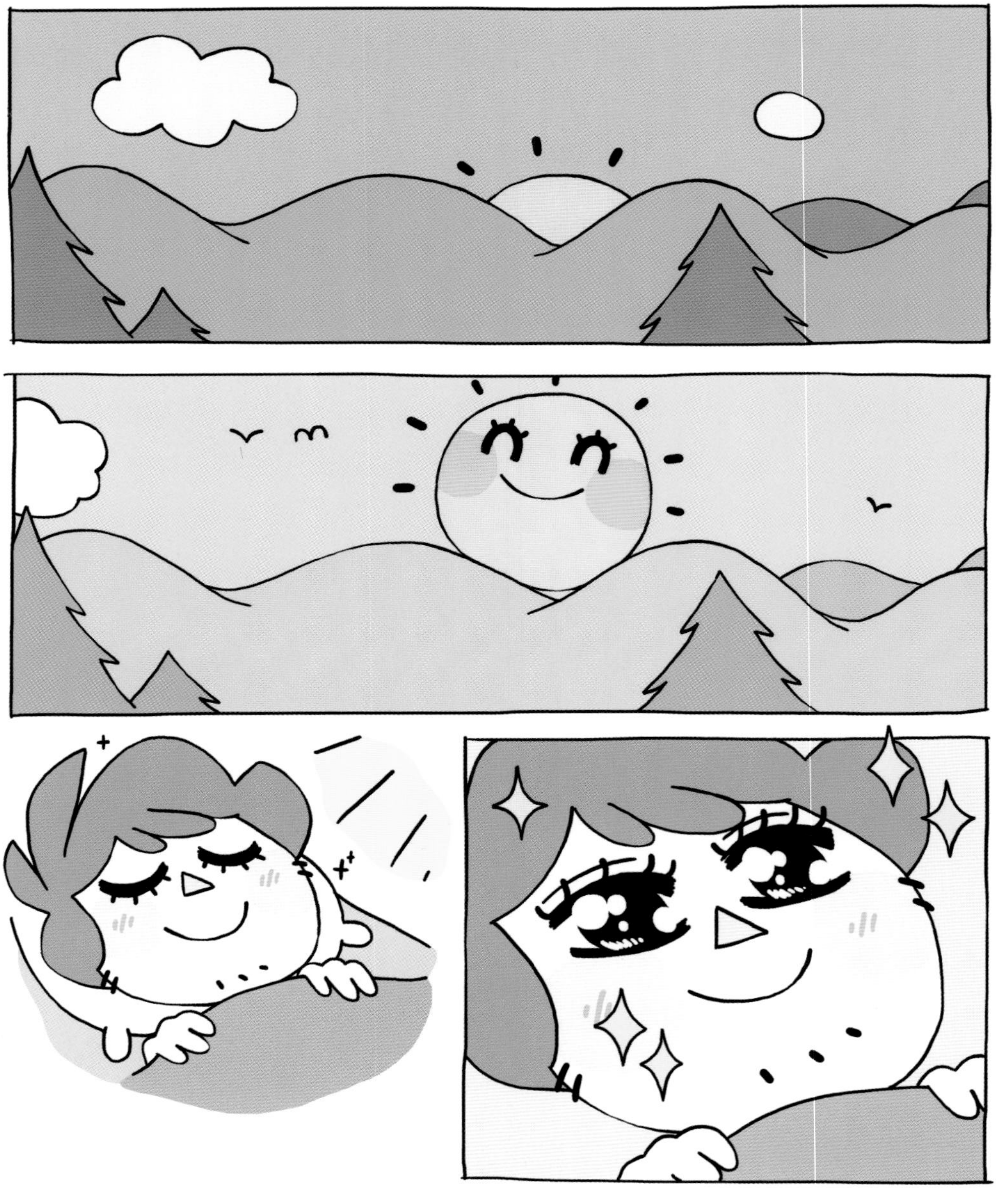

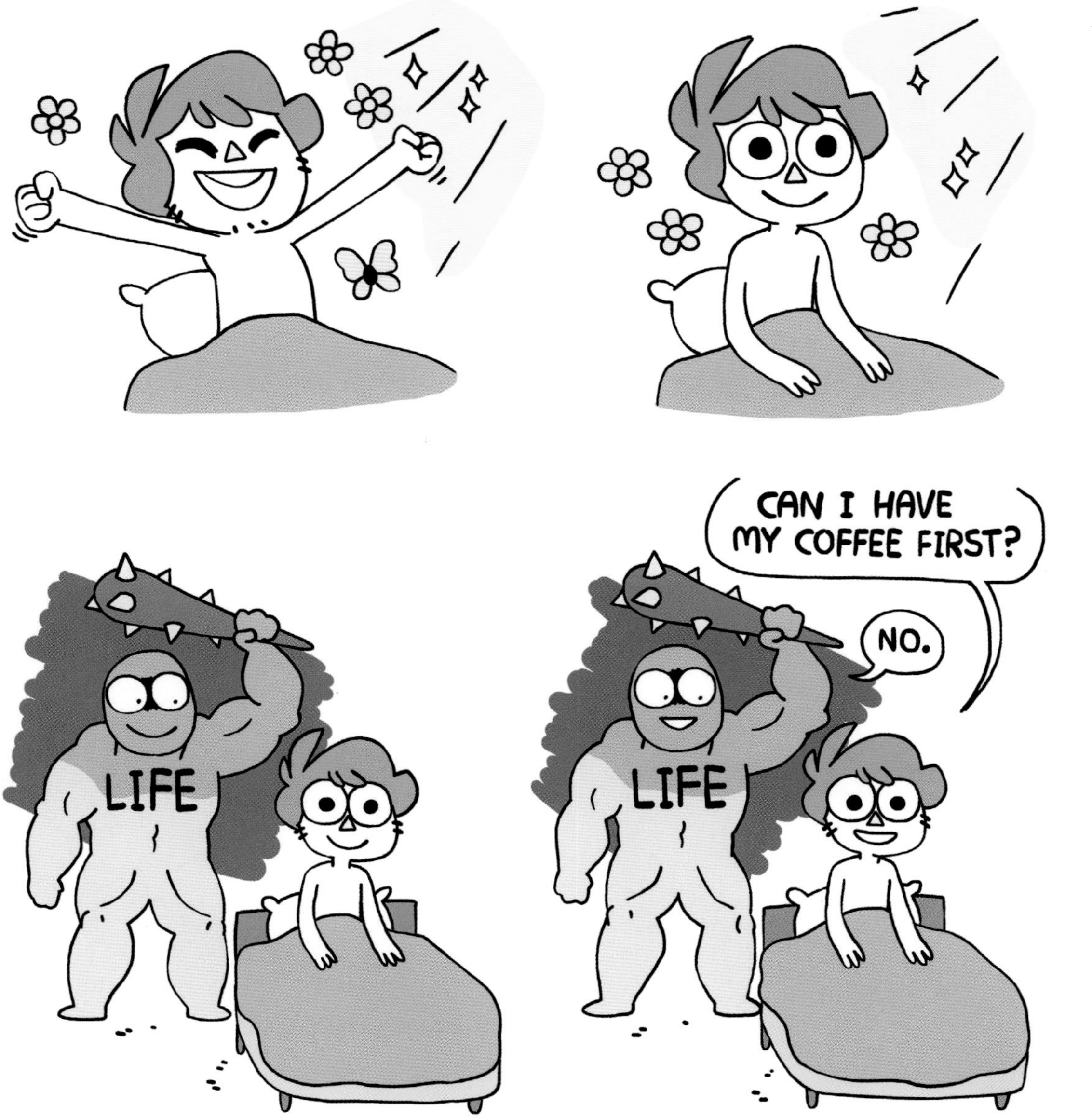
LIFE
LIFE
CAN I HAVE MY COFFEE FIRST?
NO.

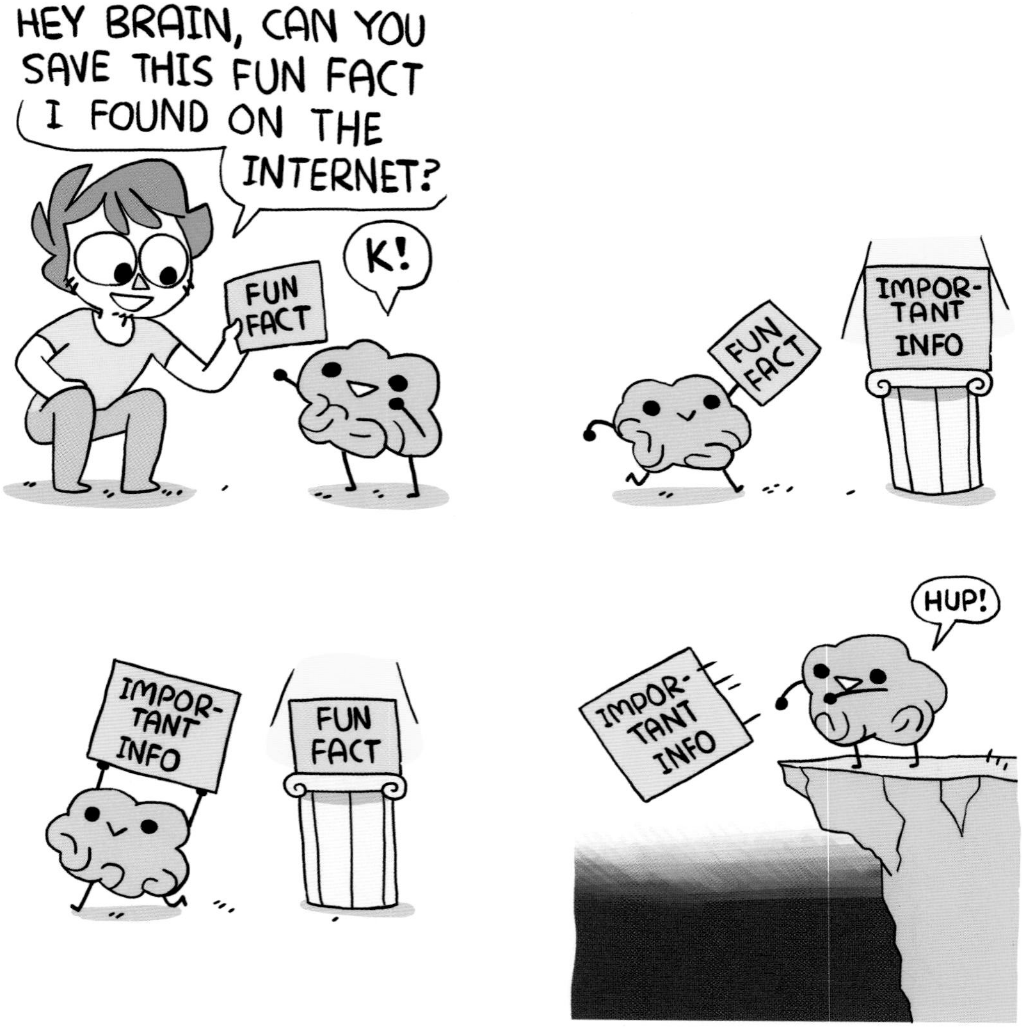
HEY BRAIN, CAN YOU SAVE THIS FUN FACT I FOUND ON THE INTERNET?
FUN FACT
K!
FUN FACT
IMPOR-TANT INFO
IMPOR-TANT INFO
FUN FACT
IMPOR-TANT INFO
HUP!

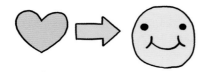

EVERYBODY KNOWS
THAT HAPPINESS
LEADS TO SMILING.

BUT DID YOU KNOW
THAT **SMILING** CAN
LEAD TO **HAPPINESS**?

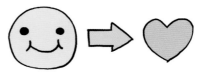

SMILING "CONVINCES"
YOUR BRAIN THAT YOU
ARE HAPPY.

THAT'S WHY I TRY
TO SMILE AS MUCH
AS POSSIBLE EVERY
SINGLE DAY!

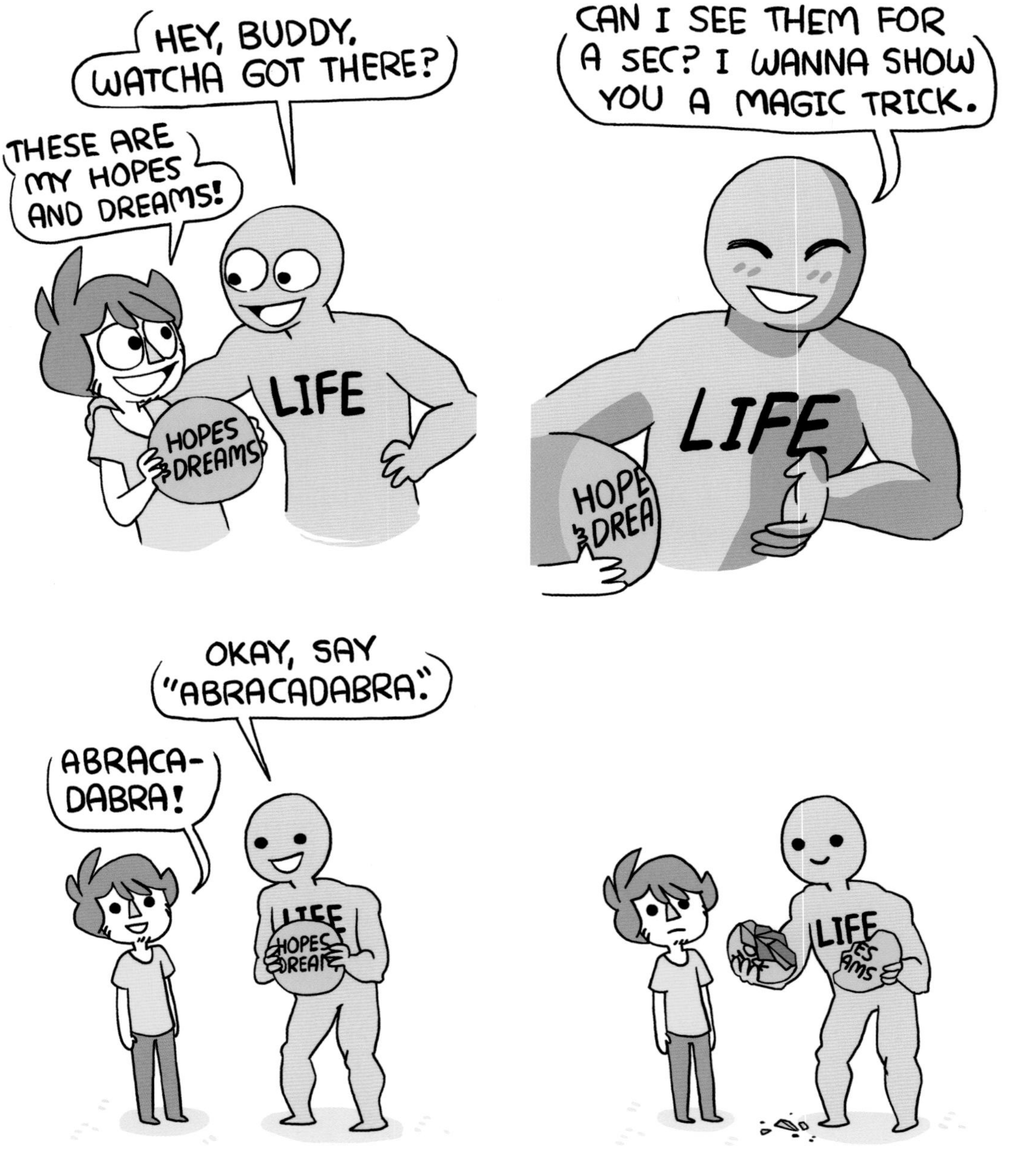
HEY, BUDDY. WATCHA GOT THERE?
THESE ARE MY HOPES AND DREAMS!
HOPES & DREAMS
LIFE
CAN I SEE THEM FOR A SEC? I WANNA SHOW YOU A MAGIC TRICK.
LIFE
OKAY, SAY "ABRACADABRA."
ABRACA-DABRA!
LIFE

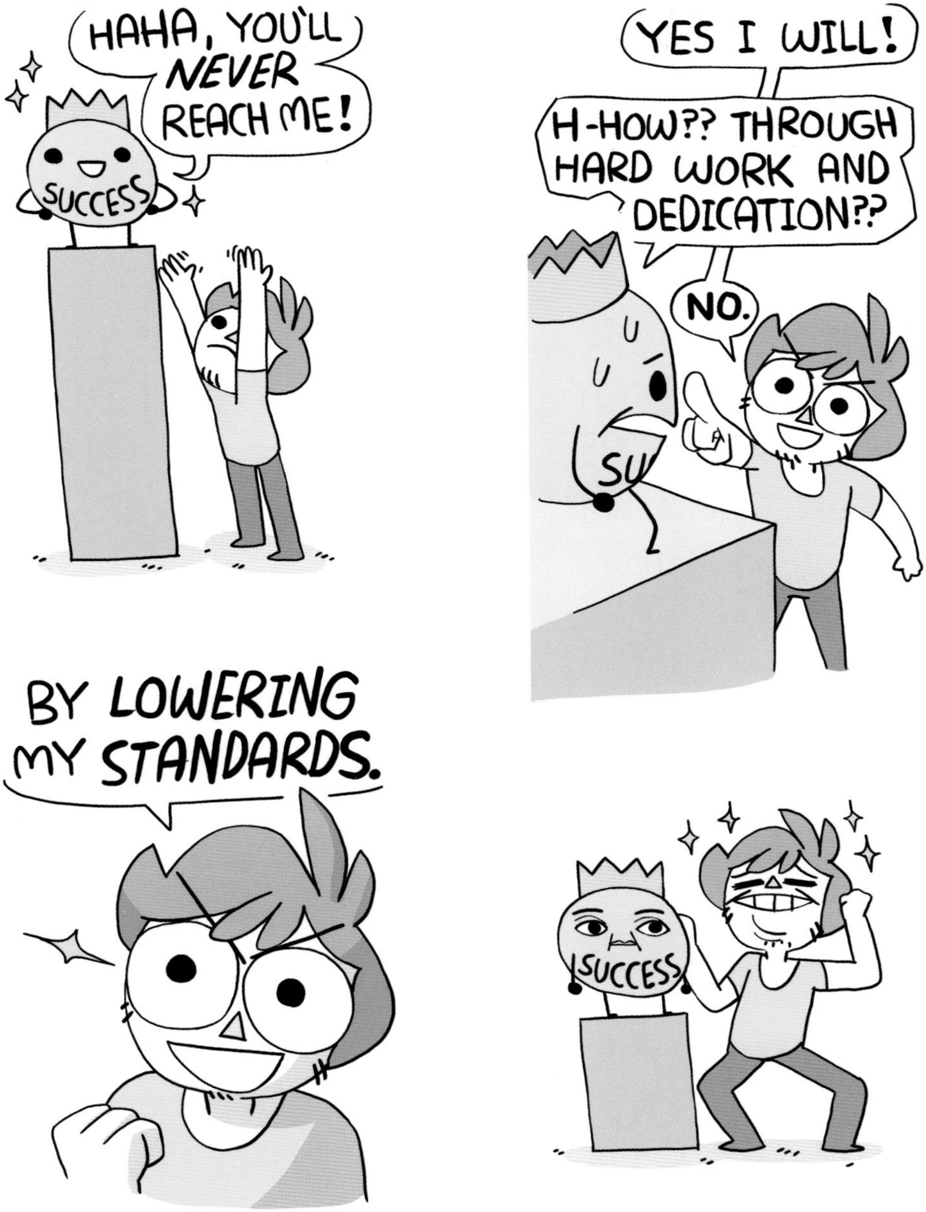
HAHA, YOU'LL NEVER REACH ME!
SUCCESS
YES I WILL!
H-HOW?? THROUGH HARD WORK AND DEDICATION??
NO.
SU
BY LOWERING MY STANDARDS.
SUCCESS

HAVE YOU EVER MET SOMEBODY WHO JUST SEEMED BETTER THAN YOU IN EVERY WAY?

IT'S OKAY! ONLY **YOU** CAN ADD WHAT YOU ADD TO THE WORLD.

PAP PAP

SO DON'T LOOK AT THEM. JUST FOCUS ON YOUR OWN STUFF!

DON'T LOOK.

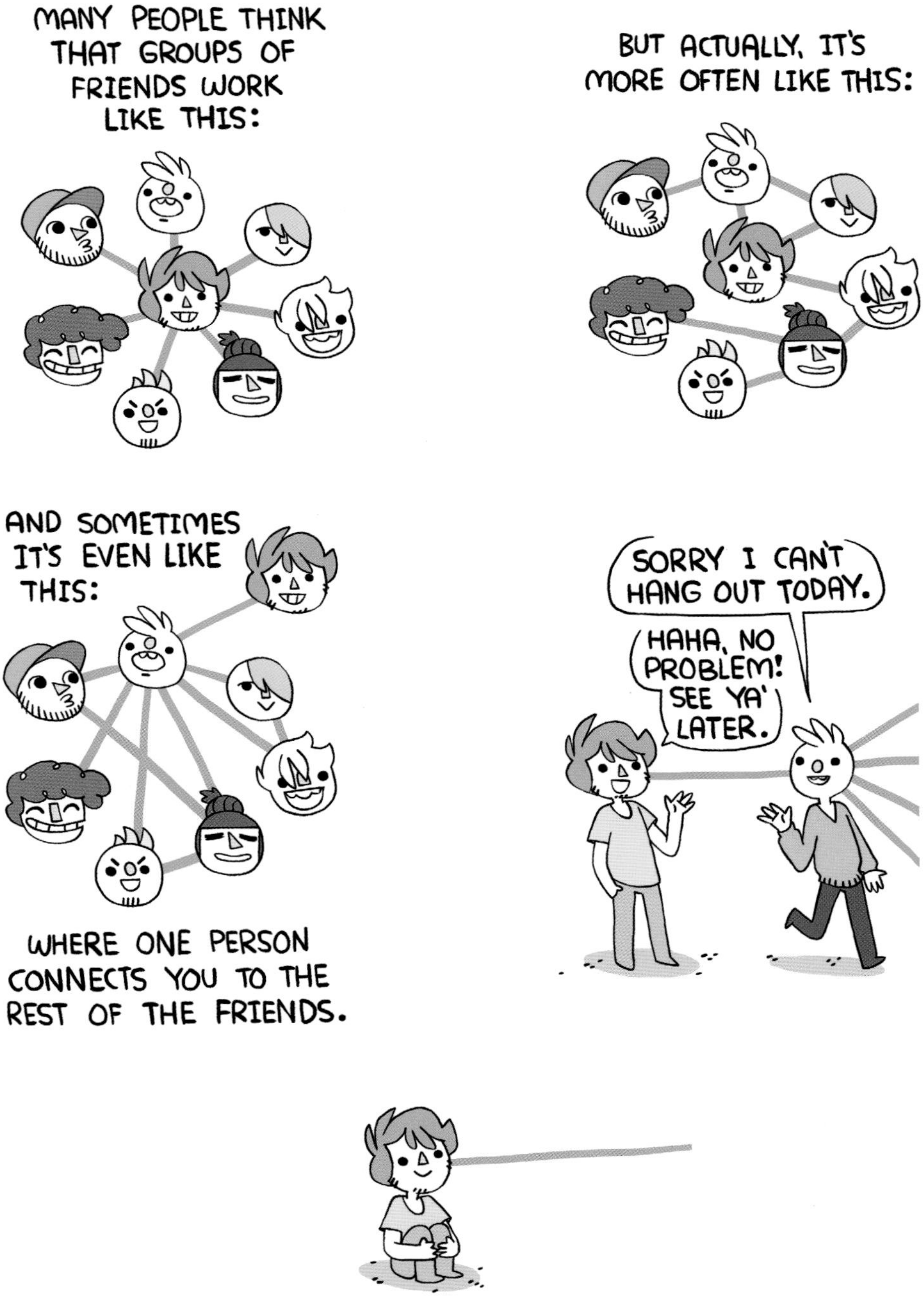
MANY PEOPLE THINK THAT GROUPS OF FRIENDS WORK LIKE THIS:
BUT ACTUALLY, IT'S MORE OFTEN LIKE THIS:
AND SOMETIMES IT'S EVEN LIKE THIS:
WHERE ONE PERSON CONNECTS YOU TO THE REST OF THE FRIENDS.
SORRY I CAN'T HANG OUT TODAY.
HAHA, NO PROBLEM! SEE YA' LATER.

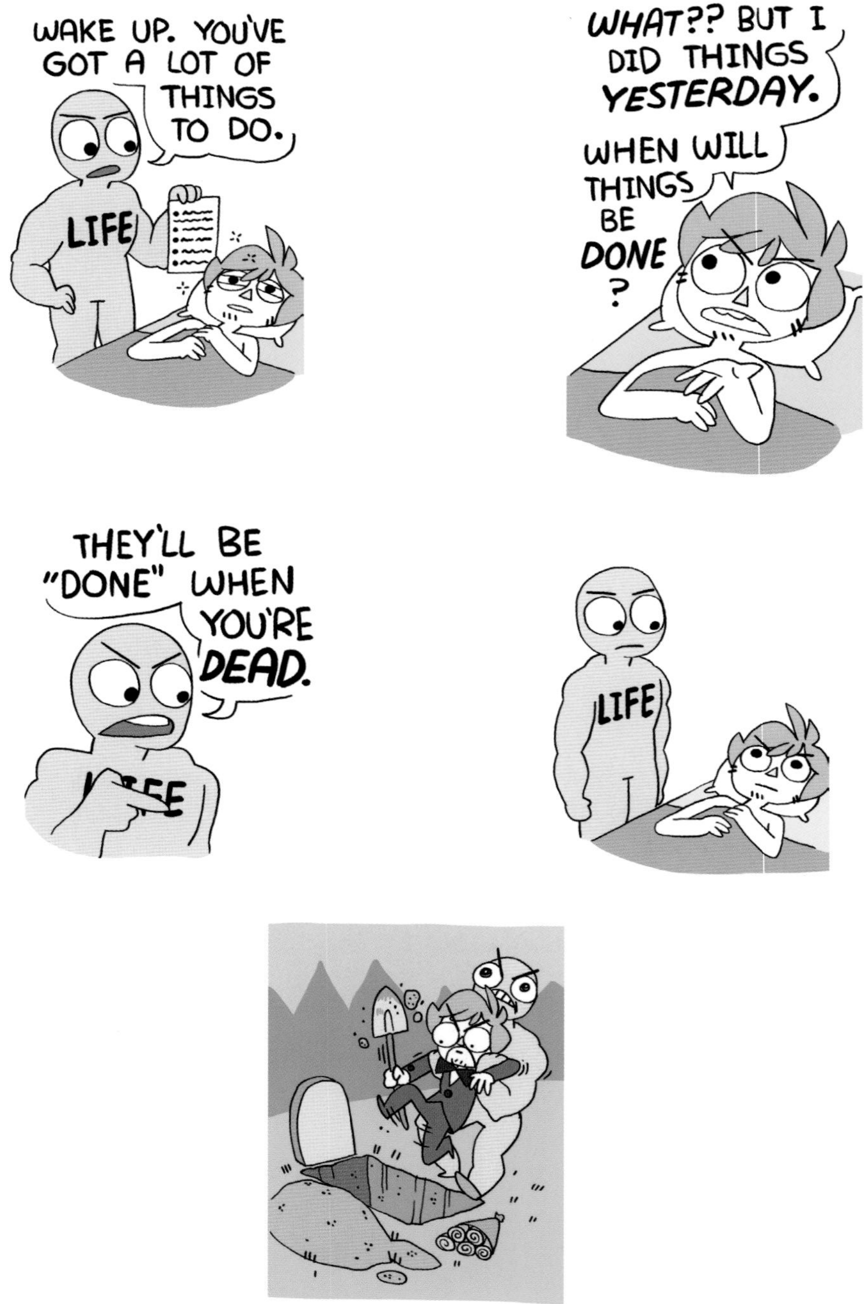
WAKE UP. YOU'VE GOT A LOT OF THINGS TO DO.
LIFE
WHAT?? BUT I DID THINGS YESTERDAY.
WHEN WILL THINGS BE DONE?
THEY'LL BE "DONE" WHEN YOU'RE DEAD.
LIFE

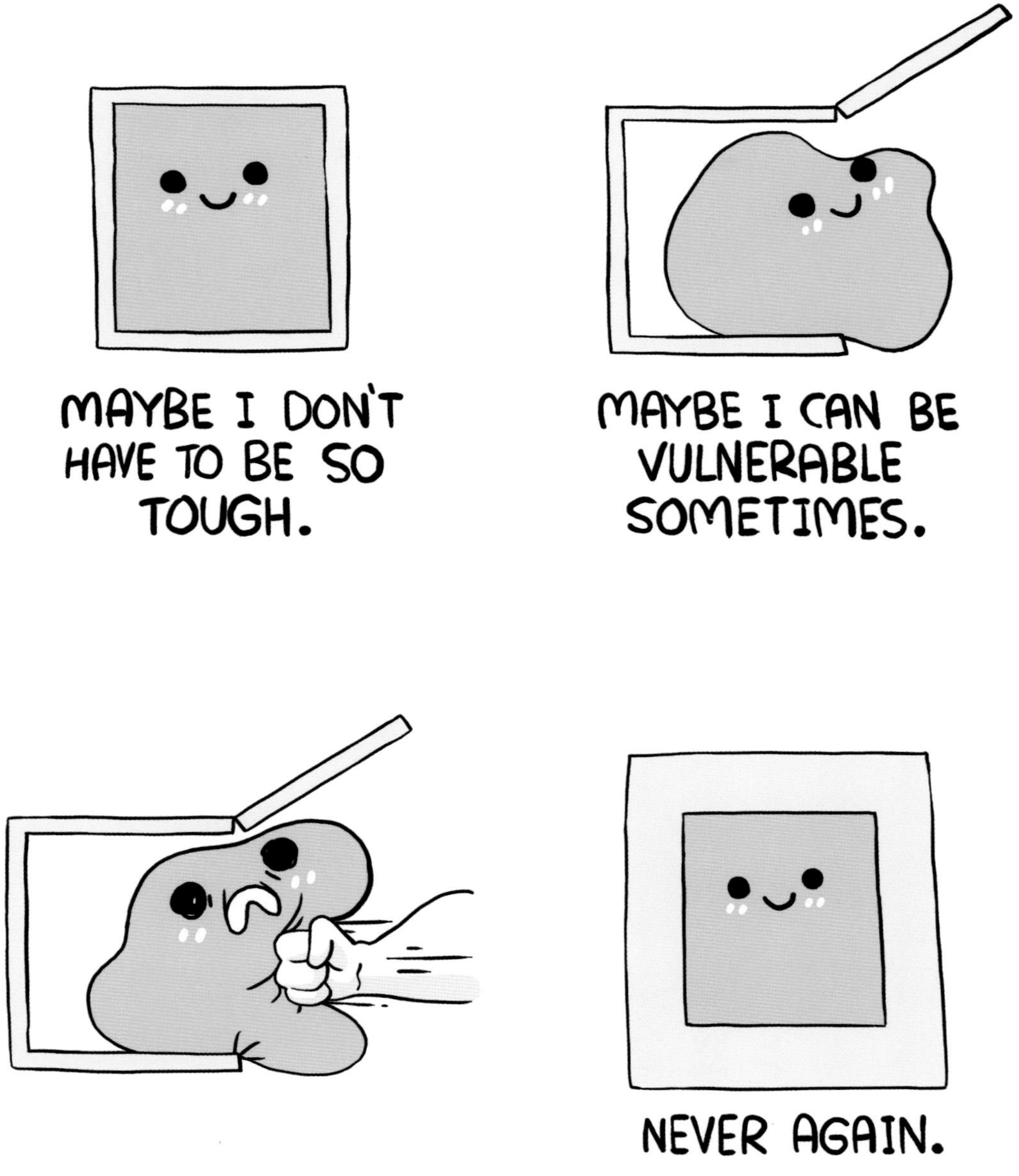
MAYBE I DON'T HAVE TO BE SO TOUGH.
MAYBE I CAN BE VULNERABLE SOMETIMES.
NEVER AGAIN.

THINGS THAT I LIKE
THINGS THAT ARE POPULAR
THINGS THAT I LIKE THAT ARE POPULAR

YOU ARE MY LAST CONNECTION TO THE WORLD OF NORMAL PEOPLE.

I WILL GUARD YOU WITH MY LIIIFE.

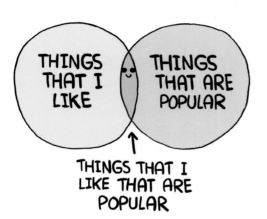

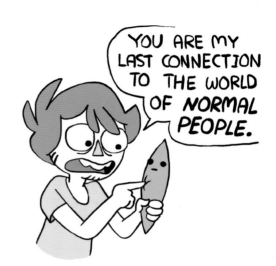

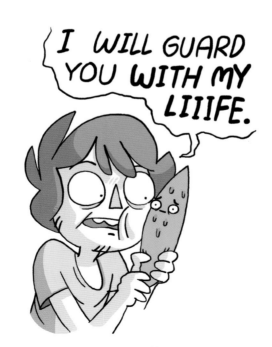

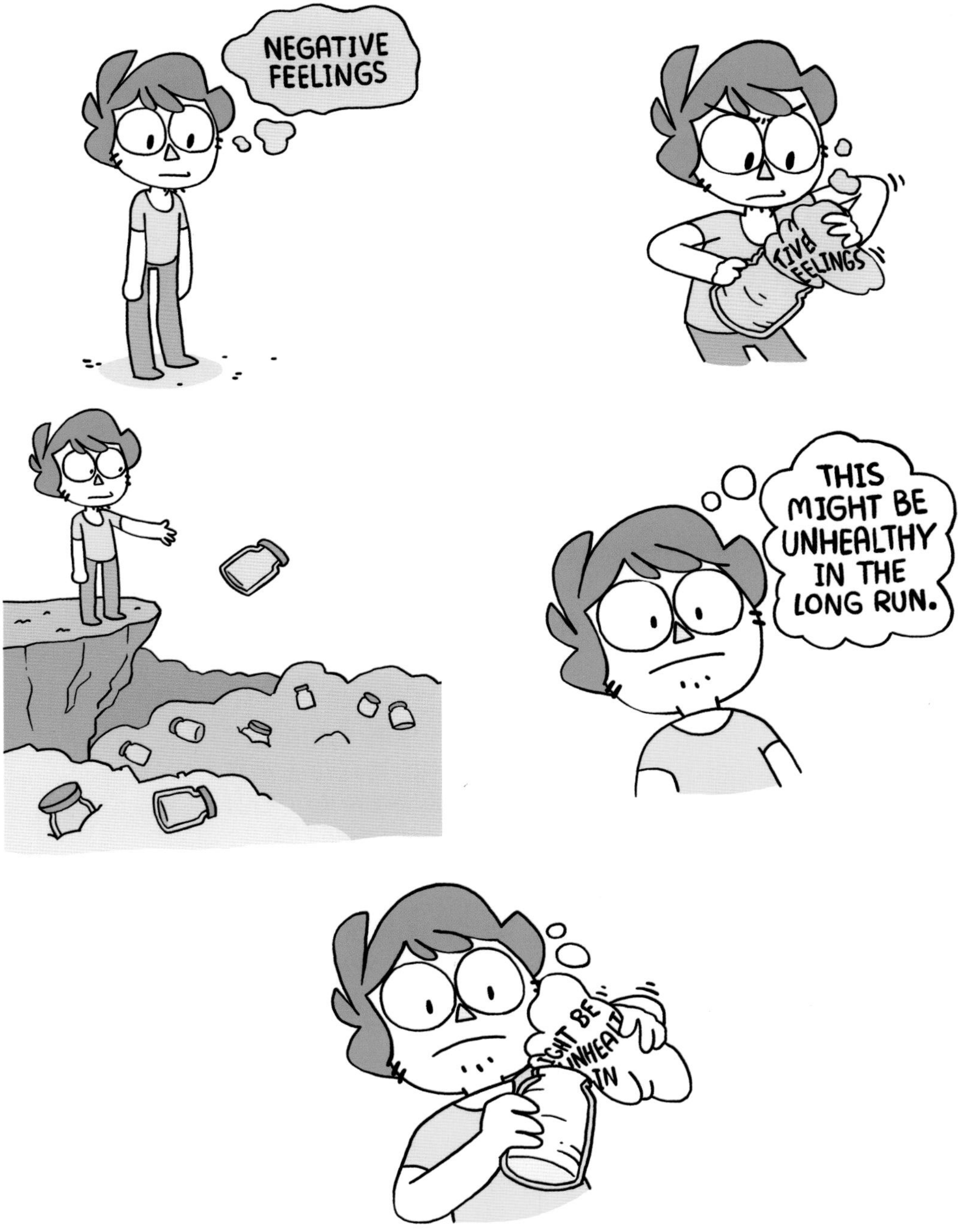
NEGATIVE FEELINGS
TIVE FEELINGS
THIS MIGHT BE UNHEALTHY IN THE LONG RUN.

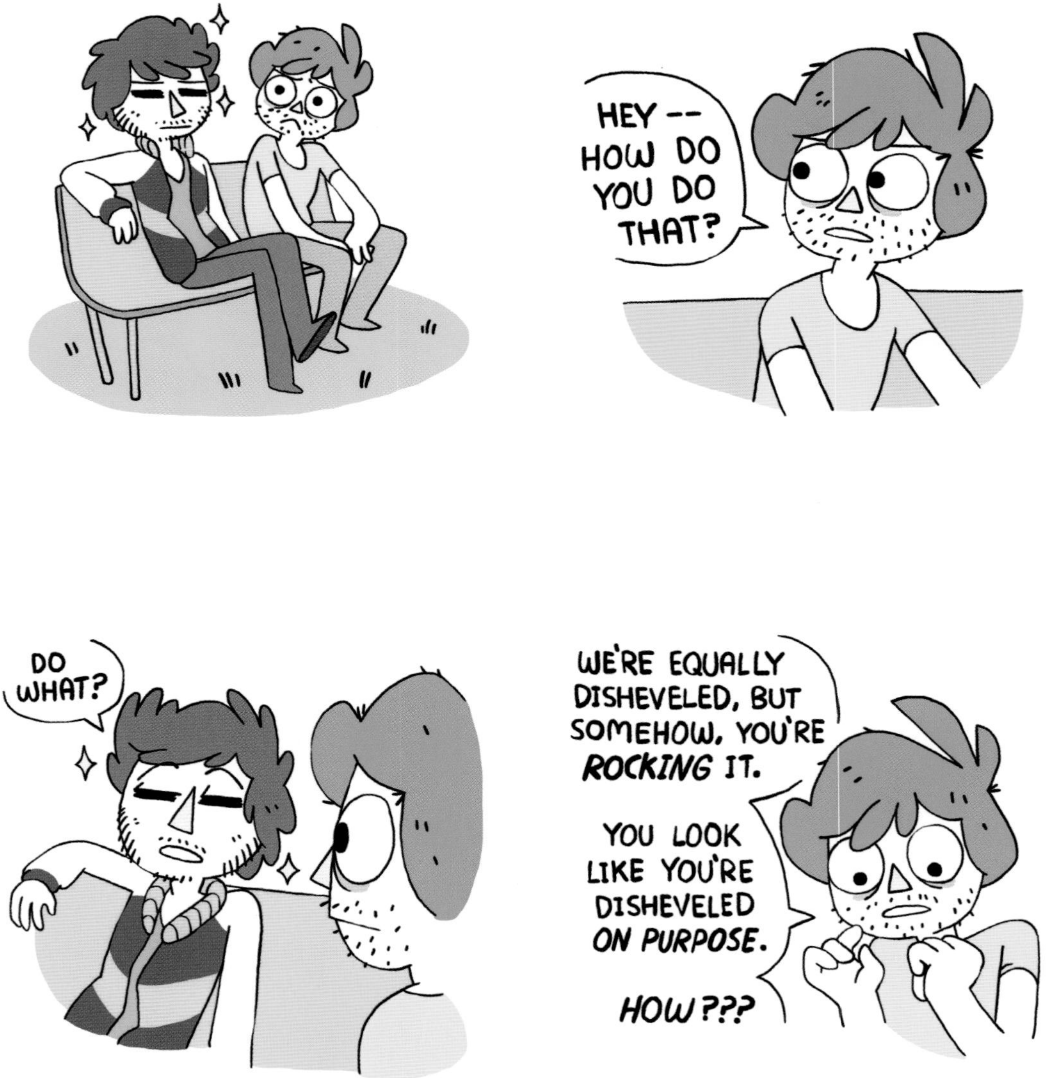
HEY -- HOW DO YOU DO THAT?
DO WHAT?
WE'RE EQUALLY DISHEVELED, BUT SOMEHOW, YOU'RE ROCKING IT.
YOU LOOK LIKE YOU'RE DISHEVELED ON PURPOSE.
HOW???

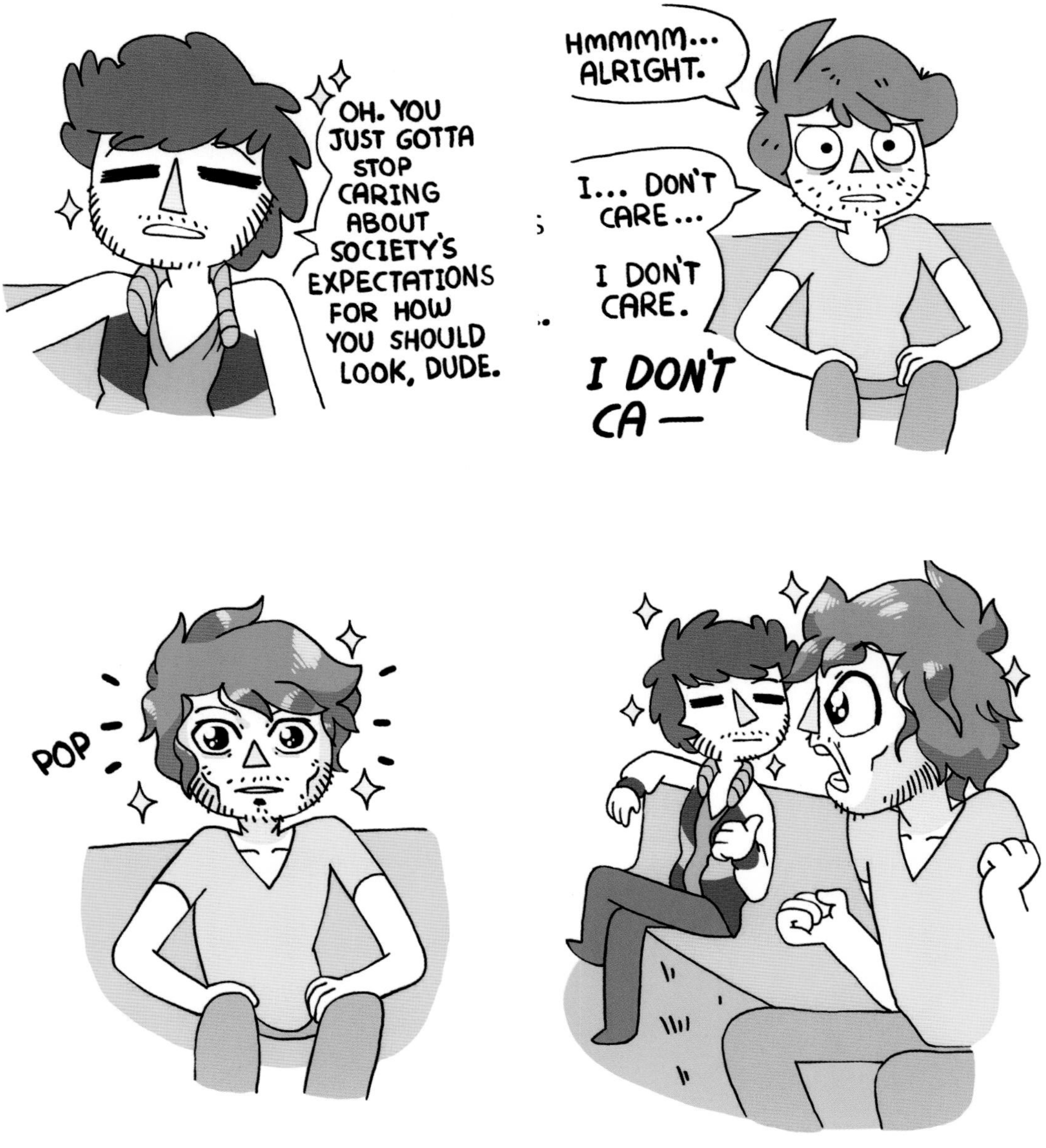
OH. YOU JUST GOTTA STOP CARING ABOUT SOCIETY'S EXPECTATIONS FOR HOW YOU SHOULD LOOK, DUDE.
HMMMM... ALRIGHT.
I... DON'T CARE...
I DON'T CARE.
I DON'T CA—
POP

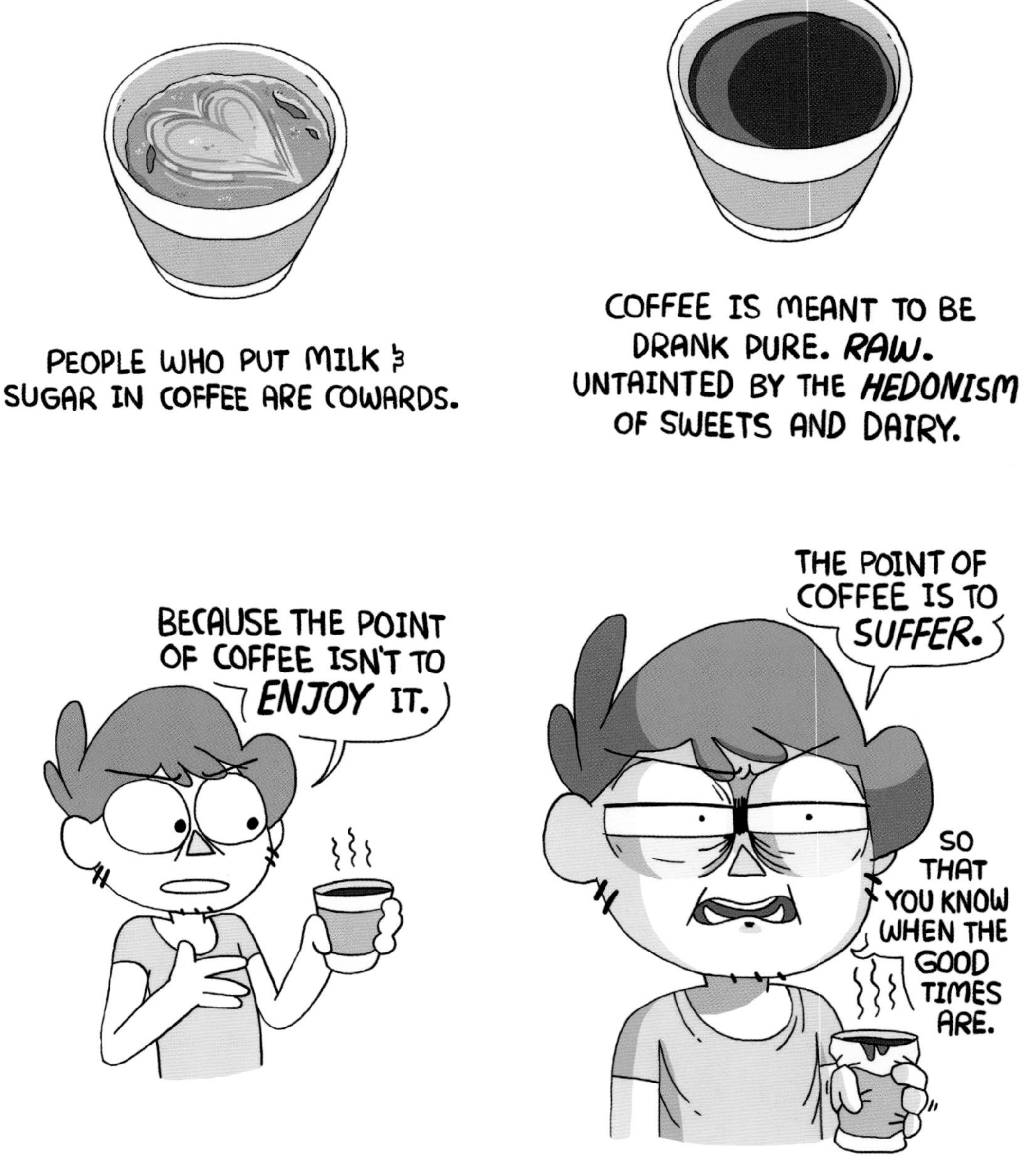
PEOPLE WHO PUT MILK & SUGAR IN COFFEE ARE COWARDS.
COFFEE IS MEANT TO BE DRANK PURE. *RAW.* UNTAINTED BY THE *HEDONISM* OF SWEETS AND DAIRY.
BECAUSE THE POINT OF COFFEE ISN'T TO *ENJOY* IT.
THE POINT OF COFFEE IS TO *SUFFER.*
SO THAT YOU KNOW WHEN THE GOOD TIMES ARE.

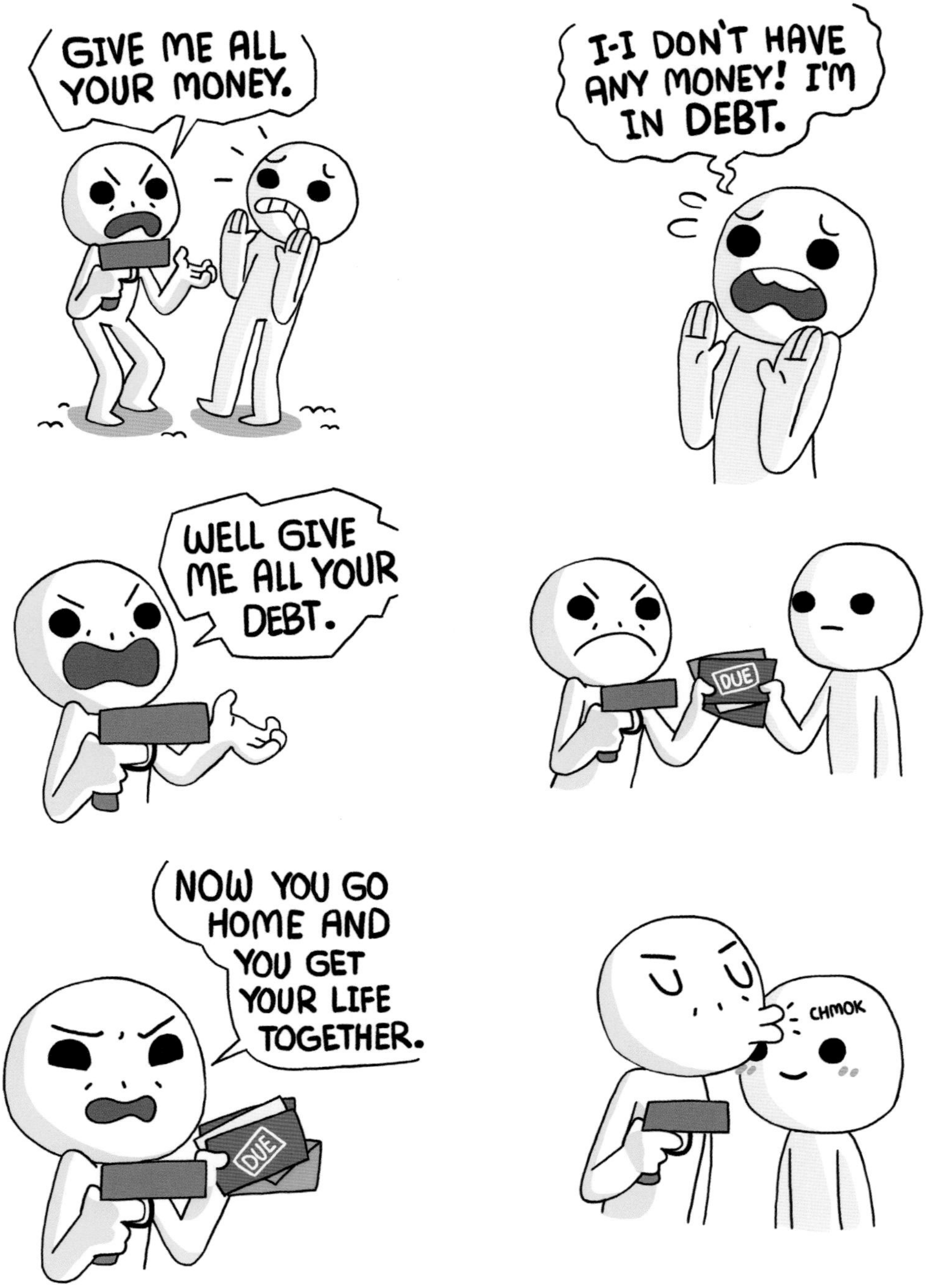
GIVE ME ALL YOUR MONEY.
I-I DON'T HAVE ANY MONEY! I'M IN DEBT.
WELL GIVE ME ALL YOUR DEBT.
DUE
NOW YOU GO HOME AND YOU GET YOUR LIFE TOGETHER.
DUE
CHMOK

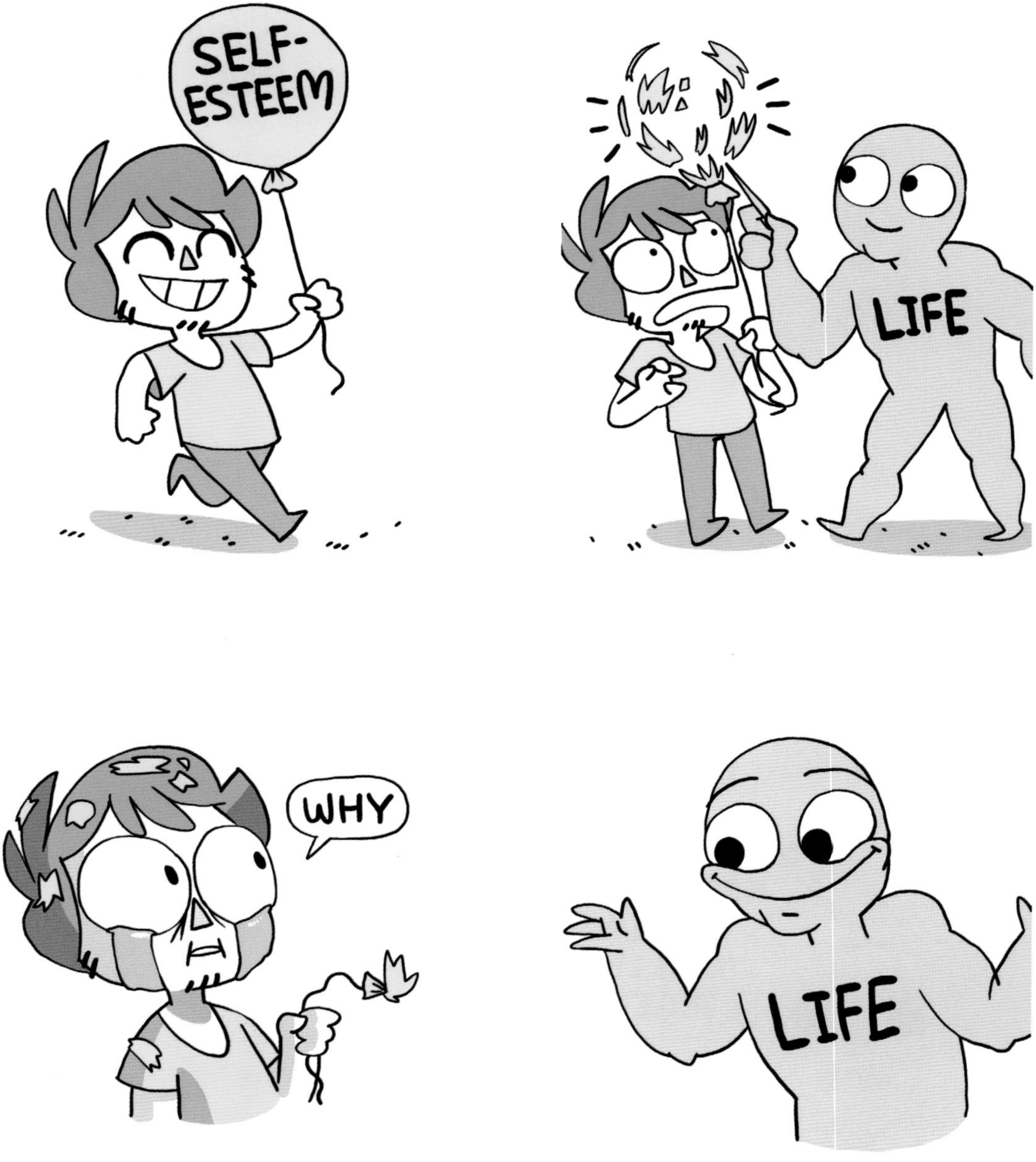
SELF-
ESTEEM
LIFE
WHY
LIFE

SEASONS IN THE NORTH

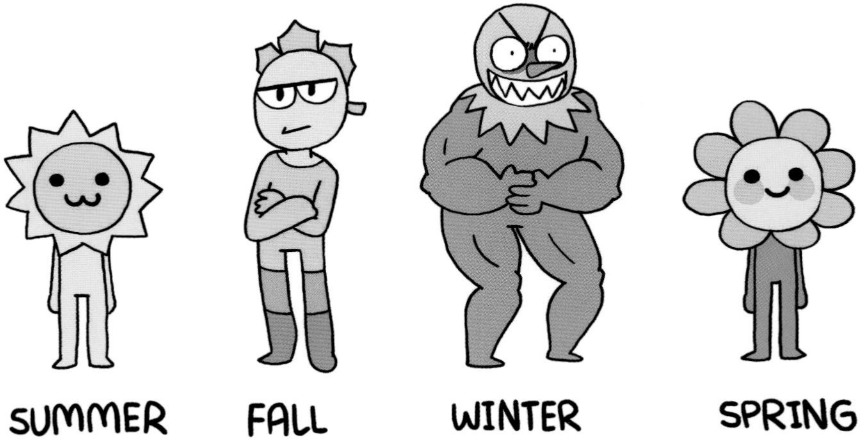
SUMMER
FALL
WINTER
SPRING

SEASONS IN THE SOUTH

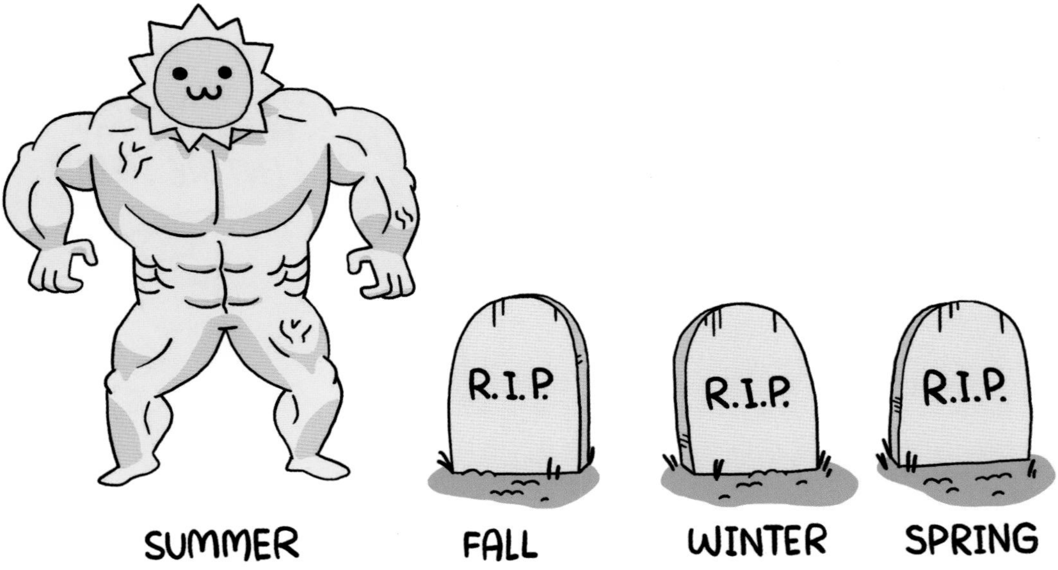
R.I.P.
R.I.P.
R.I.P.
SUMMER
FALL
WINTER
SPRING

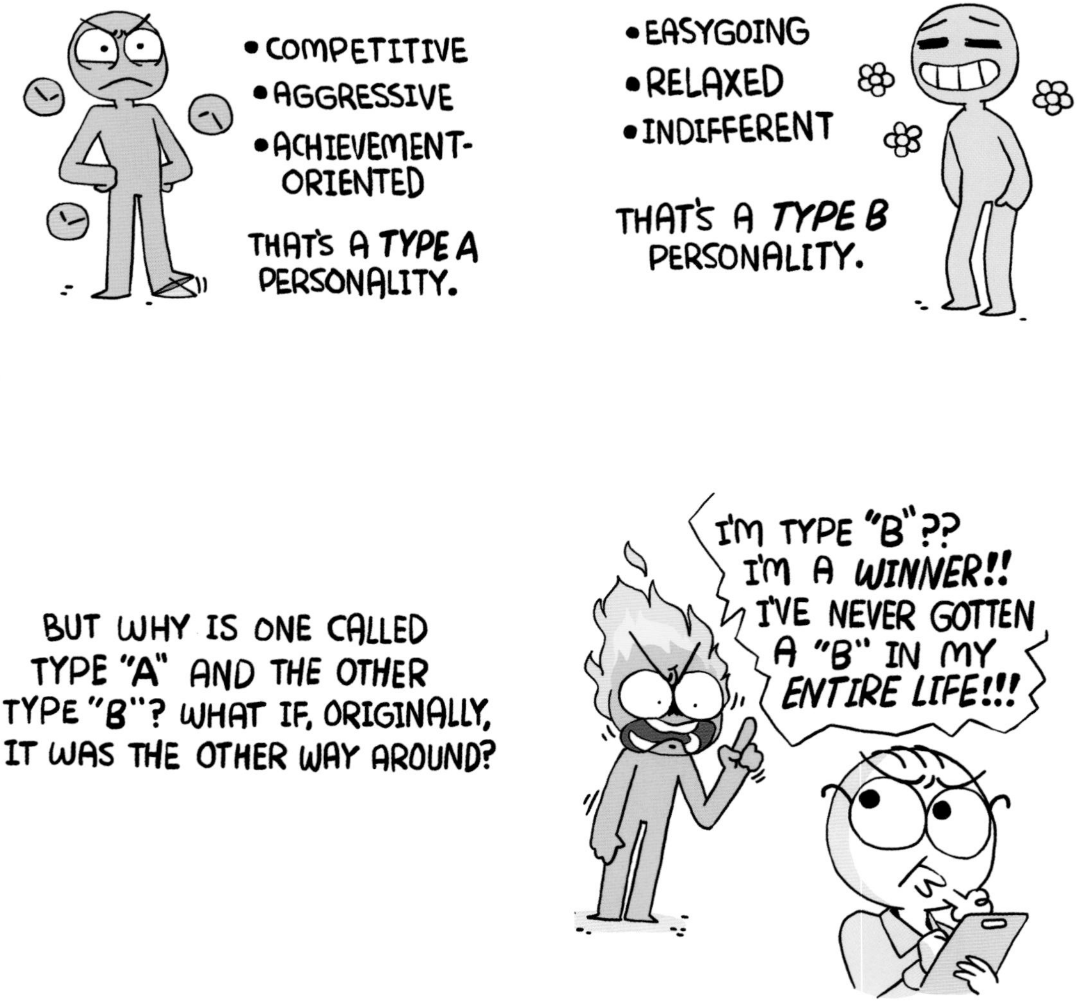
• COMPETITIVE
• AGGRESSIVE
• ACHIEVEMENT-ORIENTED
THAT'S A *TYPE A* PERSONALITY.
• EASYGOING
• RELAXED
• INDIFFERENT
THAT'S A *TYPE B* PERSONALITY.
BUT WHY IS ONE CALLED TYPE "A" AND THE OTHER TYPE "B"? WHAT IF, ORIGINALLY, IT WAS THE OTHER WAY AROUND?
I'M TYPE "B"?? I'M A *WINNER!!* I'VE NEVER GOTTEN A "B" IN MY *ENTIRE LIFE!!!*

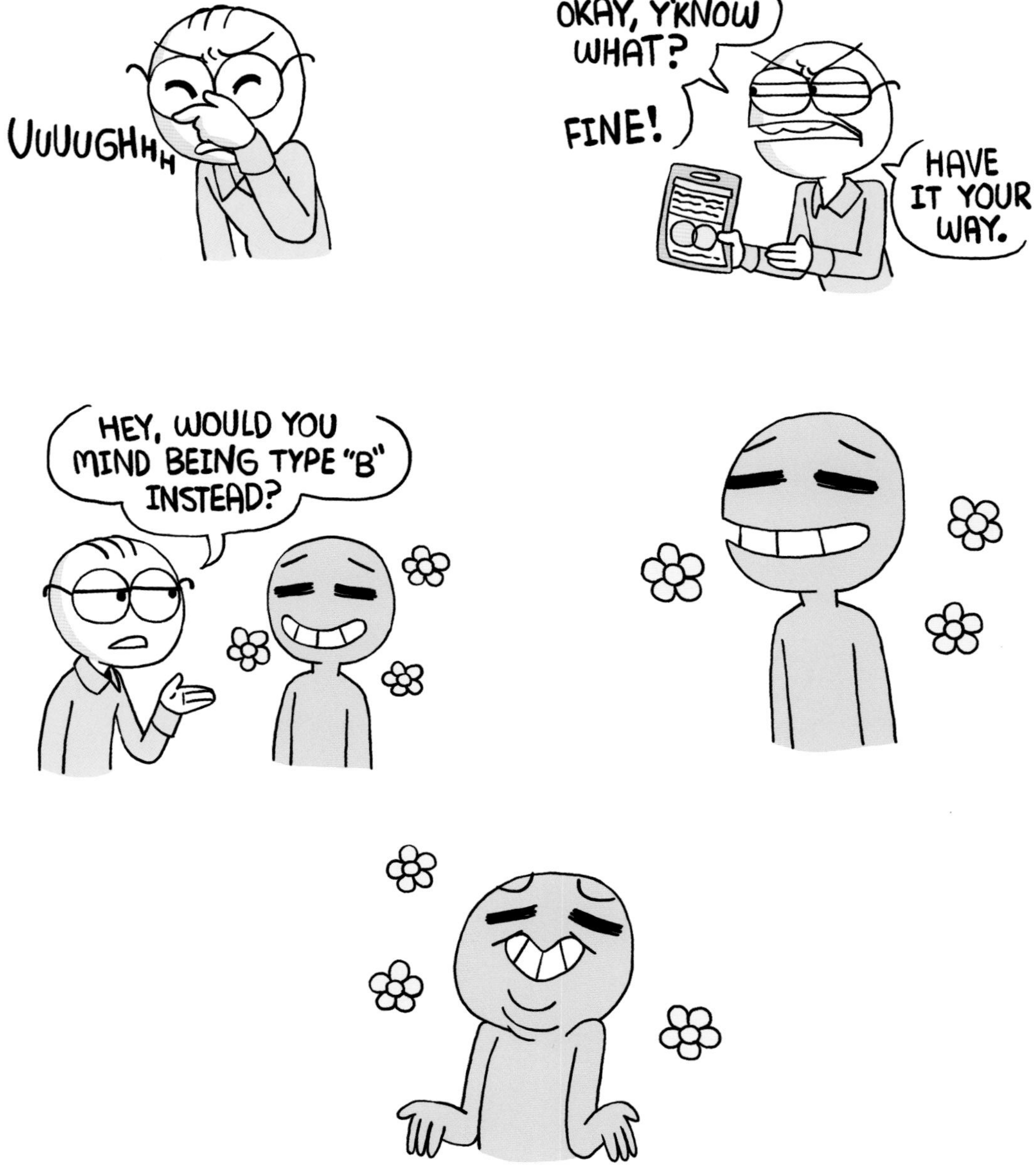
UUUUGHHHH
OKAY, Y'KNOW WHAT?
FINE!
HAVE IT YOUR WAY.
HEY, WOULD YOU MIND BEING TYPE "B" INSTEAD?

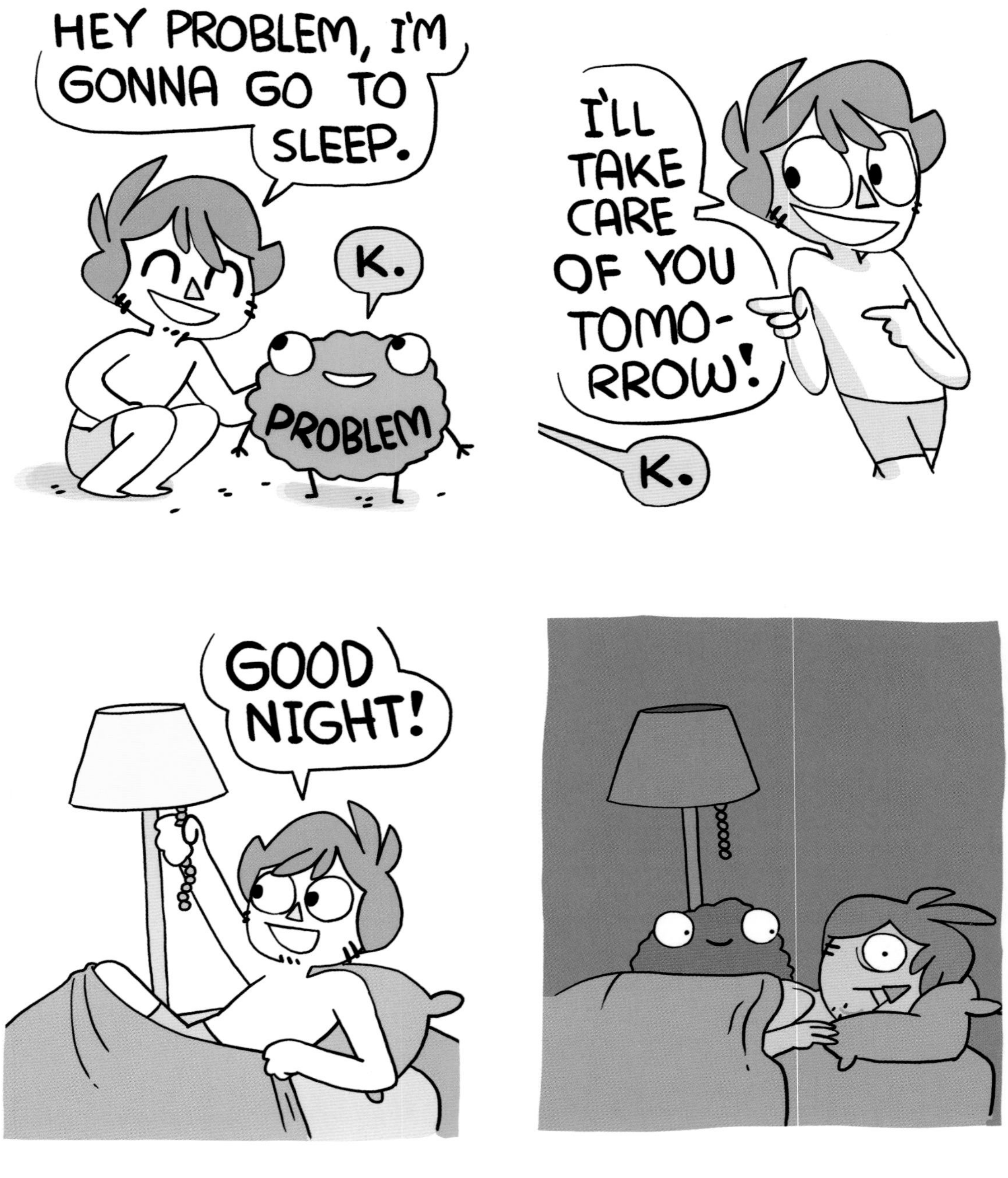
HEY PROBLEM, I'M GONNA GO TO SLEEP.
K.
PROBLEM
I'LL TAKE CARE OF YOU TOMO-RROW!
K.
GOOD NIGHT!

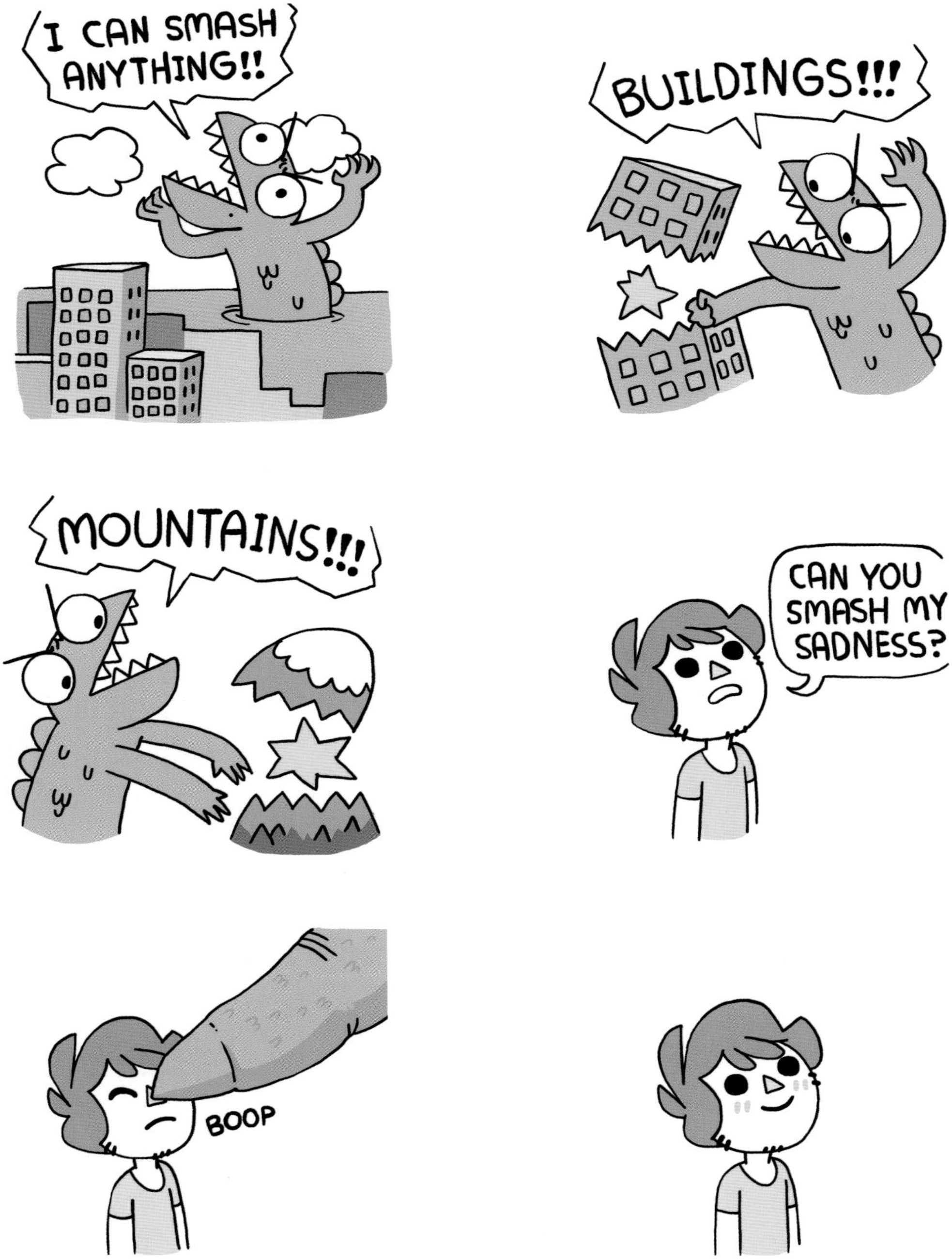
I CAN SMASH ANYTHING!!
BUILDINGS!!!
MOUNTAINS!!!
CAN YOU SMASH MY SADNESS?
BOOP

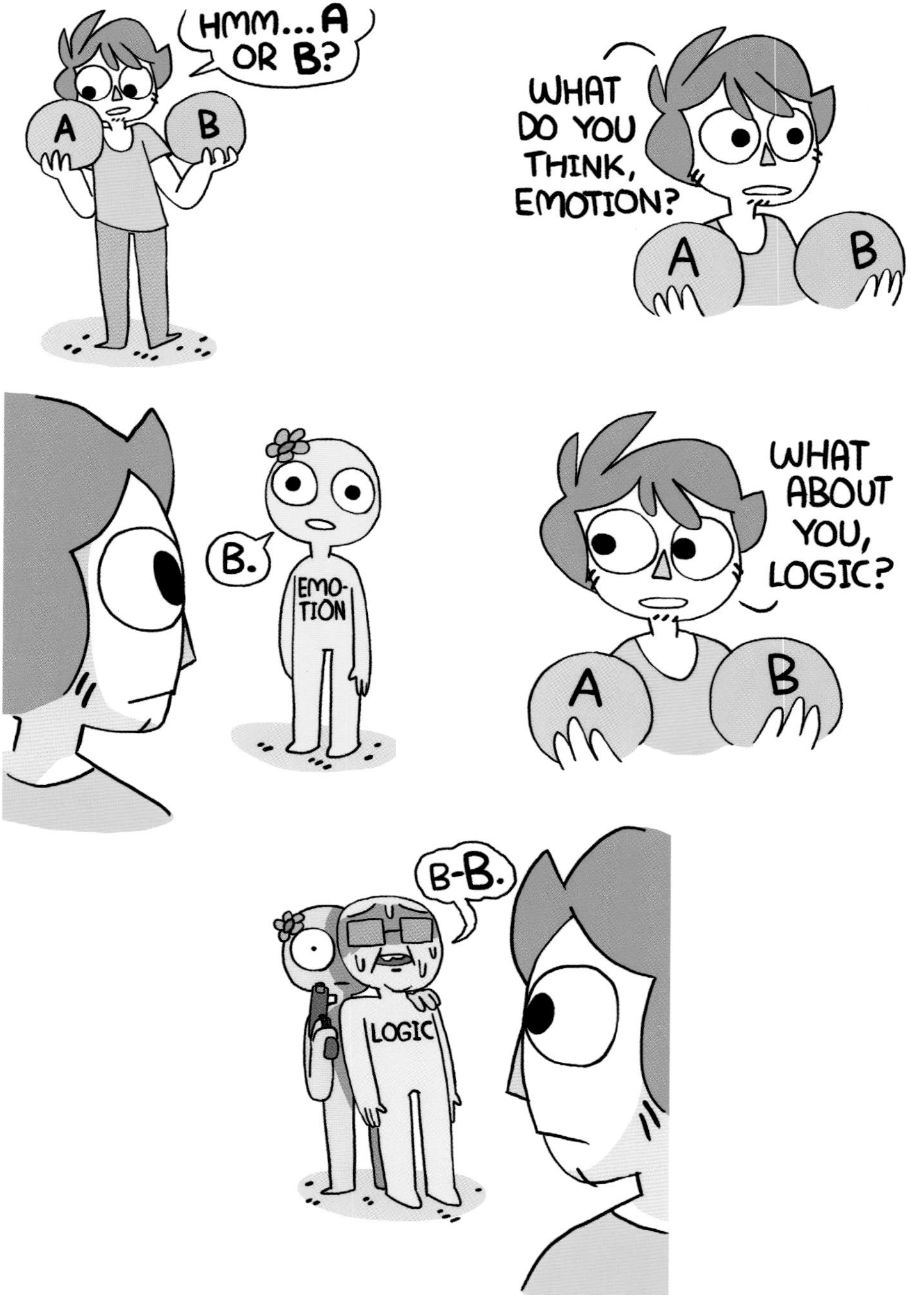
HMM...A OR B?
A
B
WHAT DO YOU THINK, EMOTION?
A
B
B.
EMO-TION
WHAT ABOUT YOU, LOGIC?
A
B
B-B.
LOGIC

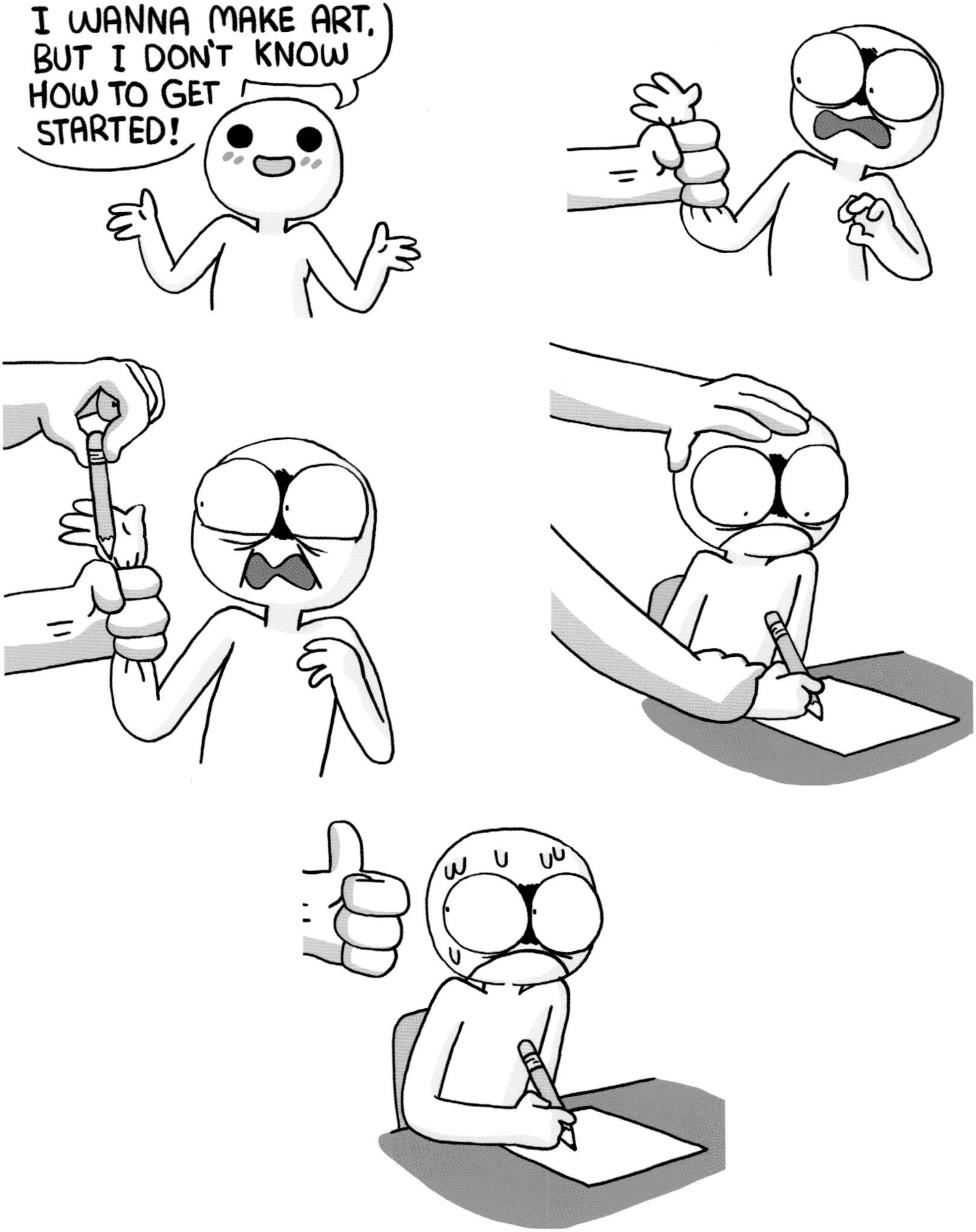
I WANNA MAKE ART, BUT I DON'T KNOW HOW TO GET STARTED!

OPTIMISTIC
APPROACH TO LIFE

PESSIMISTIC
APPROACH TO LIFE

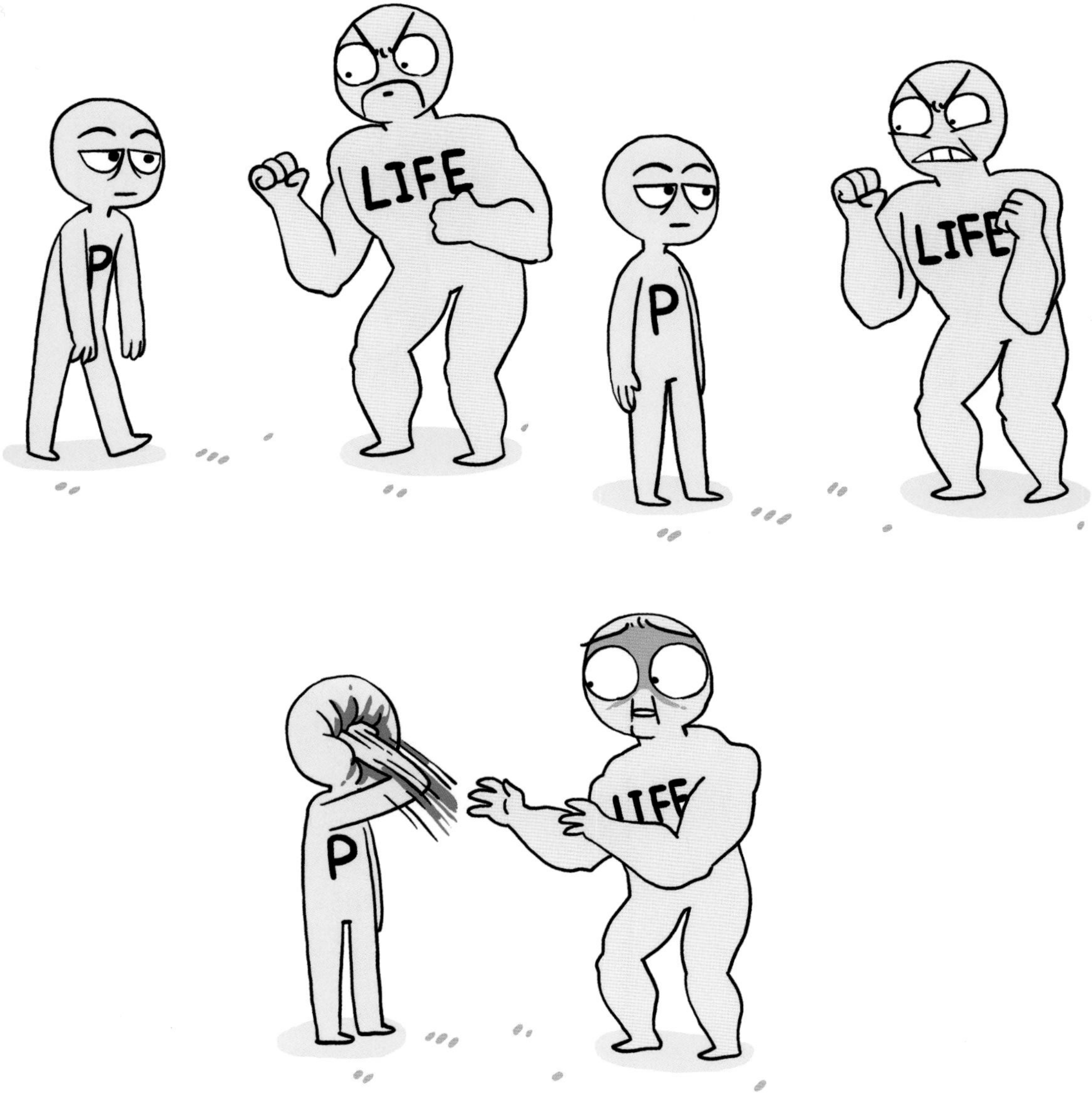
P
LIFE
P
LIFE
P
LIFE

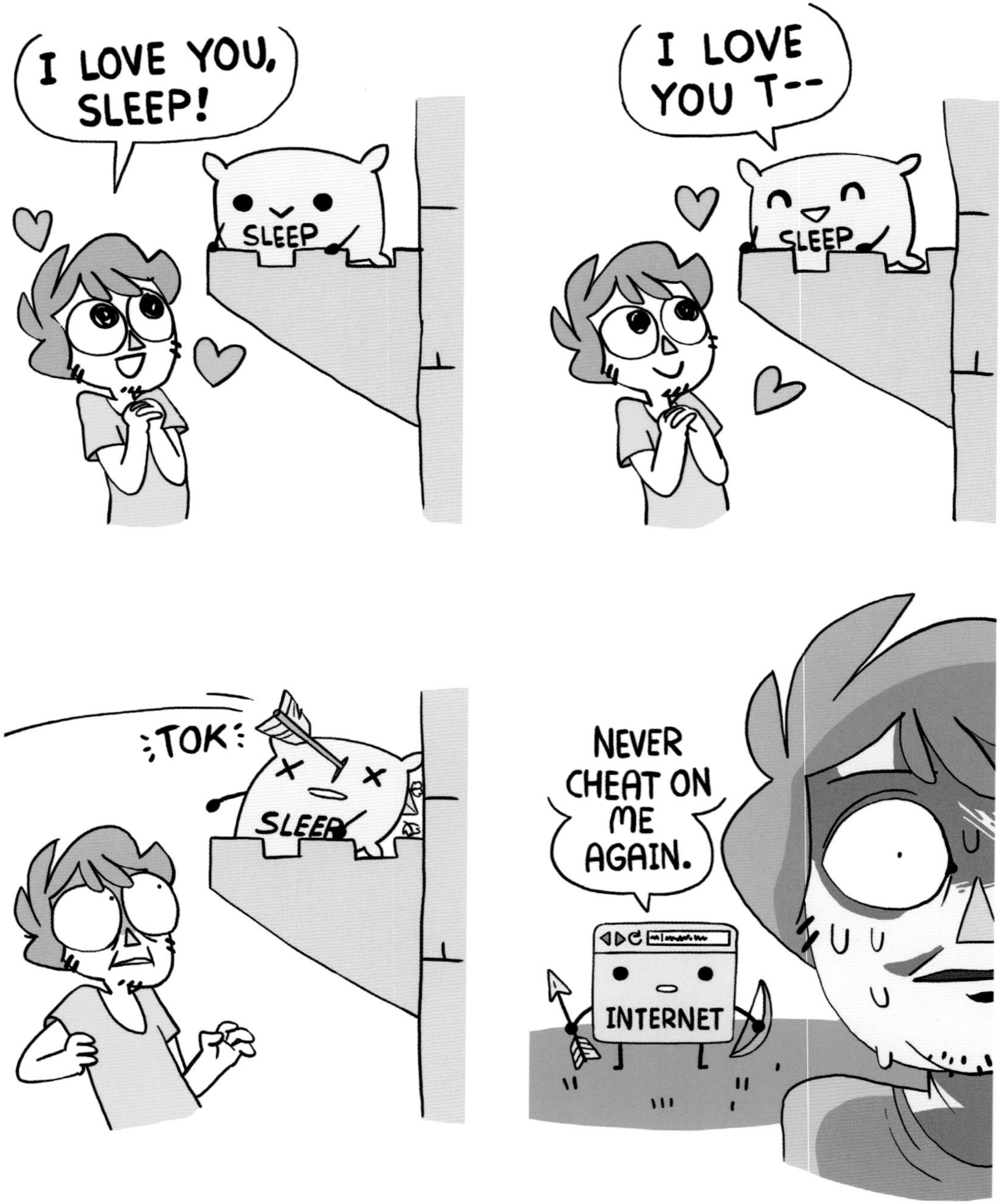
I LOVE YOU, SLEEP!
SLEEP
I LOVE YOU T--
SLEEP
TOK
SLEEP
NEVER CHEAT ON ME AGAIN.
INTERNET

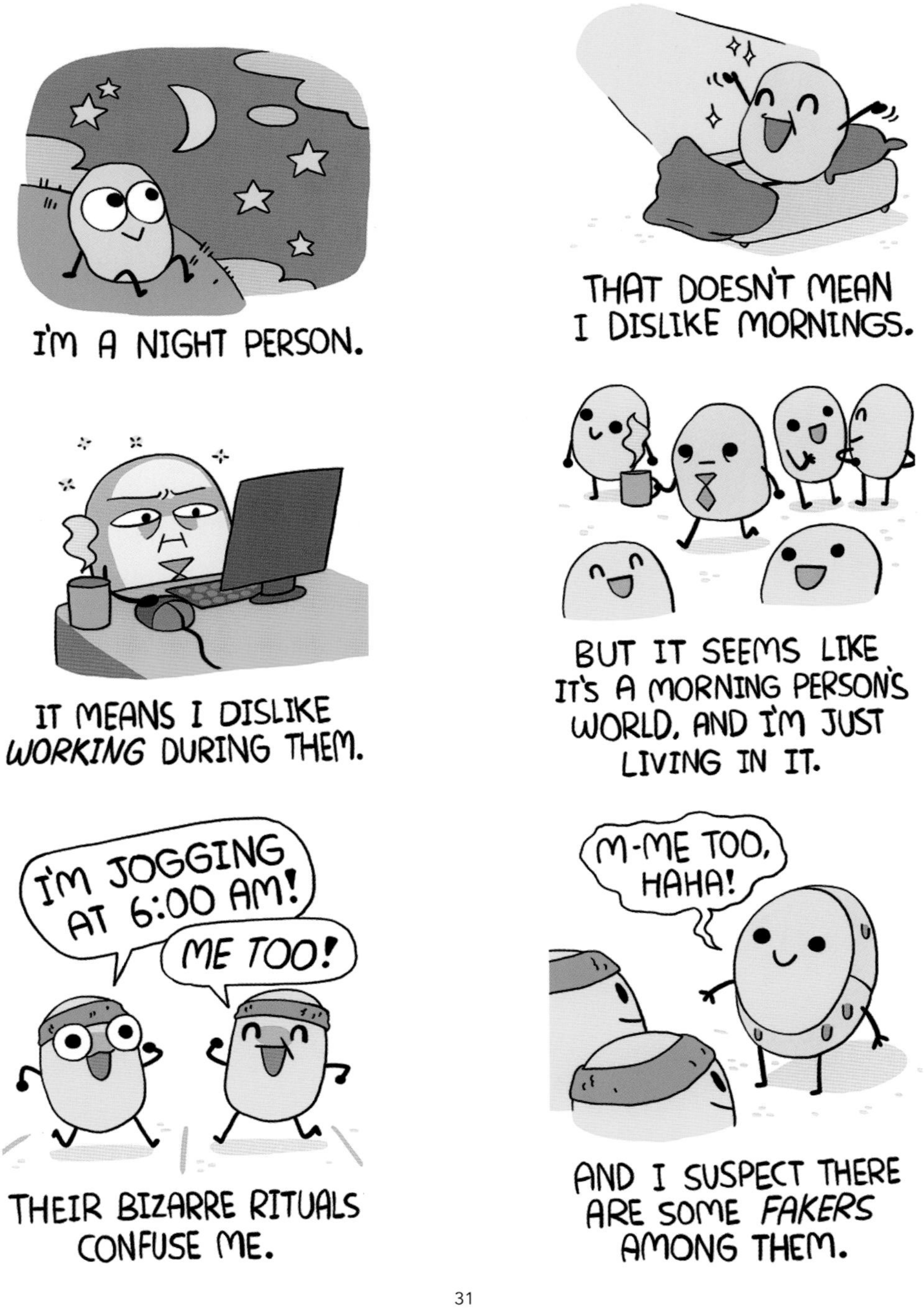
I'M A NIGHT PERSON.
THAT DOESN'T MEAN I DISLIKE MORNINGS.
IT MEANS I DISLIKE *WORKING* DURING THEM.
BUT IT SEEMS LIKE IT'S A MORNING PERSON'S WORLD, AND I'M JUST LIVING IN IT.
I'M JOGGING AT 6:00 AM!
ME TOO!
THEIR BIZARRE RITUALS CONFUSE ME.
M-ME TOO, HAHA!
AND I SUSPECT THERE ARE SOME *FAKERS* AMONG THEM.

END
MORNING
CULTURE

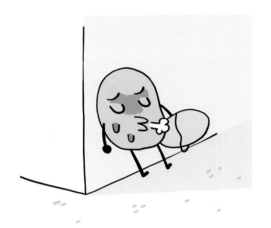

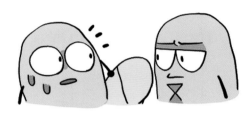

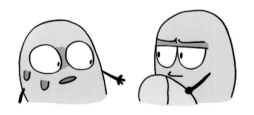

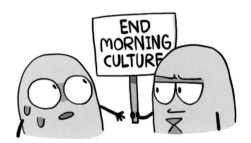

6:00 AM

THEY SAY THE EARLY
BIRD GETS THE WORM.

4:00 AM

BUT THEY DON'T KNOW
ABOUT THE REALLY,
REALLY LATE BIRD.

LOVE YOURSELF,
NIGHT PEOPLE.

GET THAT WORM.

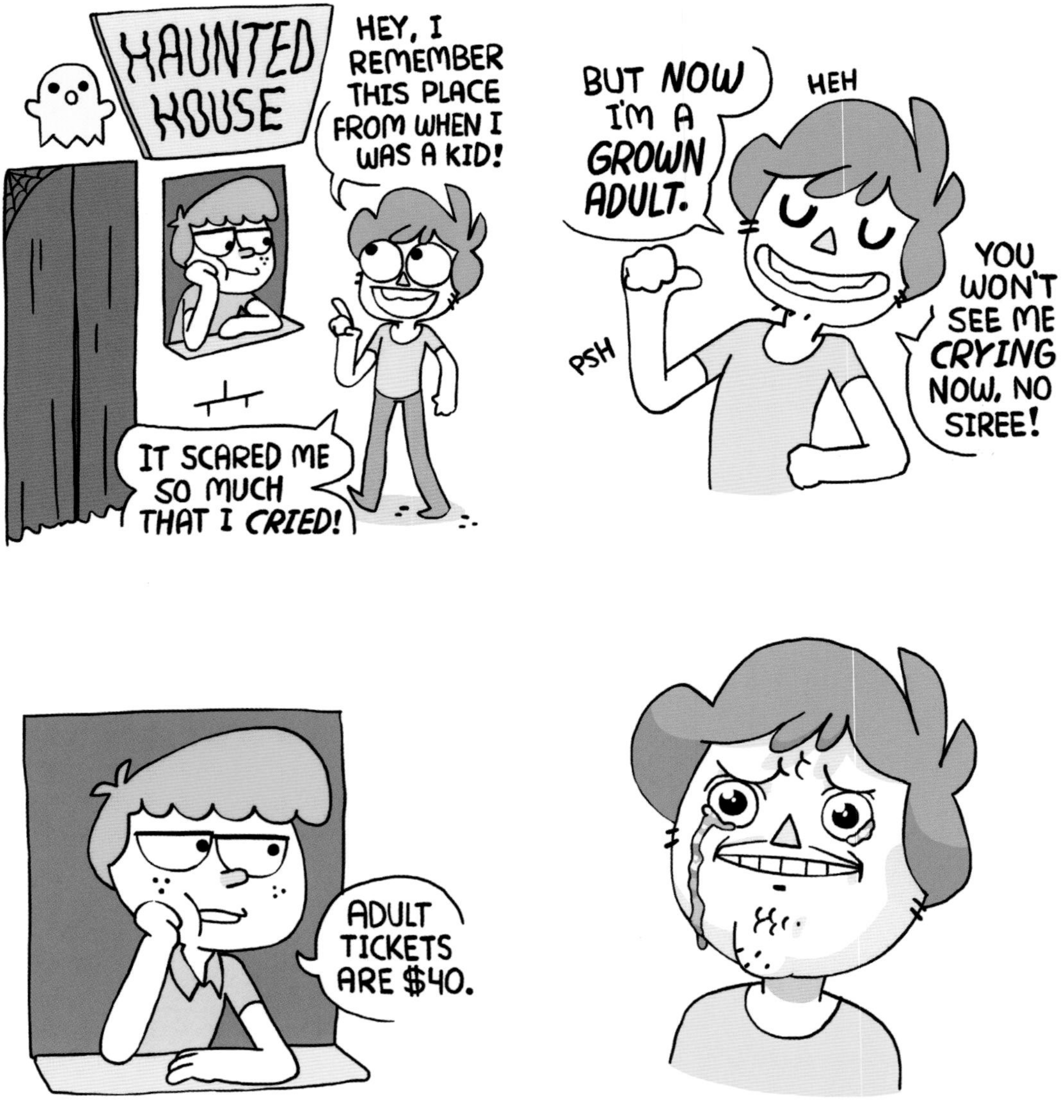
HAUNTED HOUSE
HEY, I REMEMBER THIS PLACE FROM WHEN I WAS A KID!
IT SCARED ME SO MUCH THAT I CRIED!
BUT NOW I'M A GROWN ADULT.
HEH
PSH
YOU WON'T SEE ME CRYING NOW, NO SIREE!
ADULT TICKETS ARE $40.

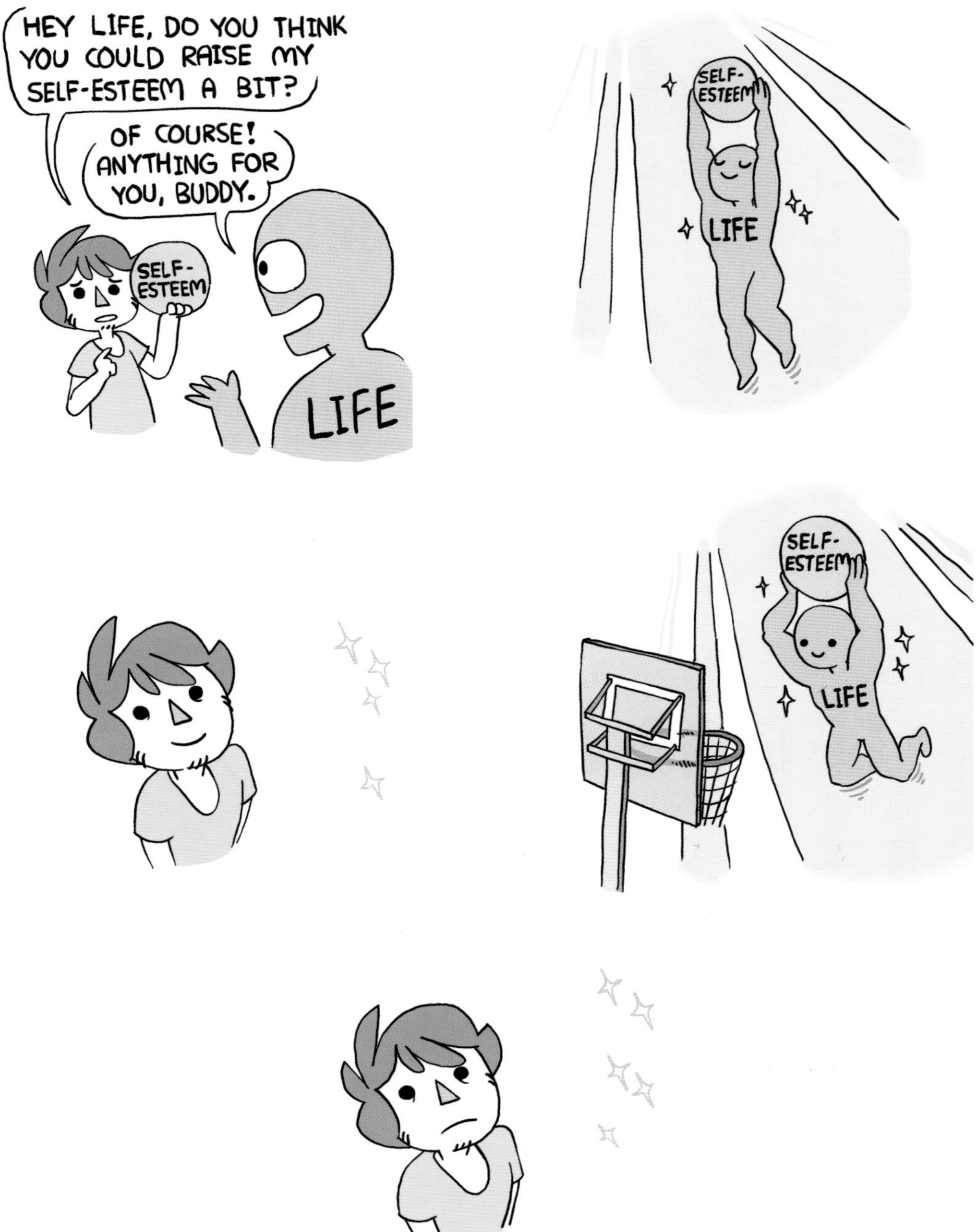
HEY LIFE, DO YOU THINK YOU COULD RAISE MY SELF-ESTEEM A BIT?
OF COURSE! ANYTHING FOR YOU, BUDDY.
SELF-ESTEEM
LIFE
SELF-ESTEEM
LIFE
SELF-ESTEEM
LIFE

RIGHT HAND

- WRITER
- ARTIST
- GREAT DEXTERITY & STRENGTH

LEFT HAND

- HAS TROUBLE WITH DOOR KNOBS
- TRIES HIS BEST

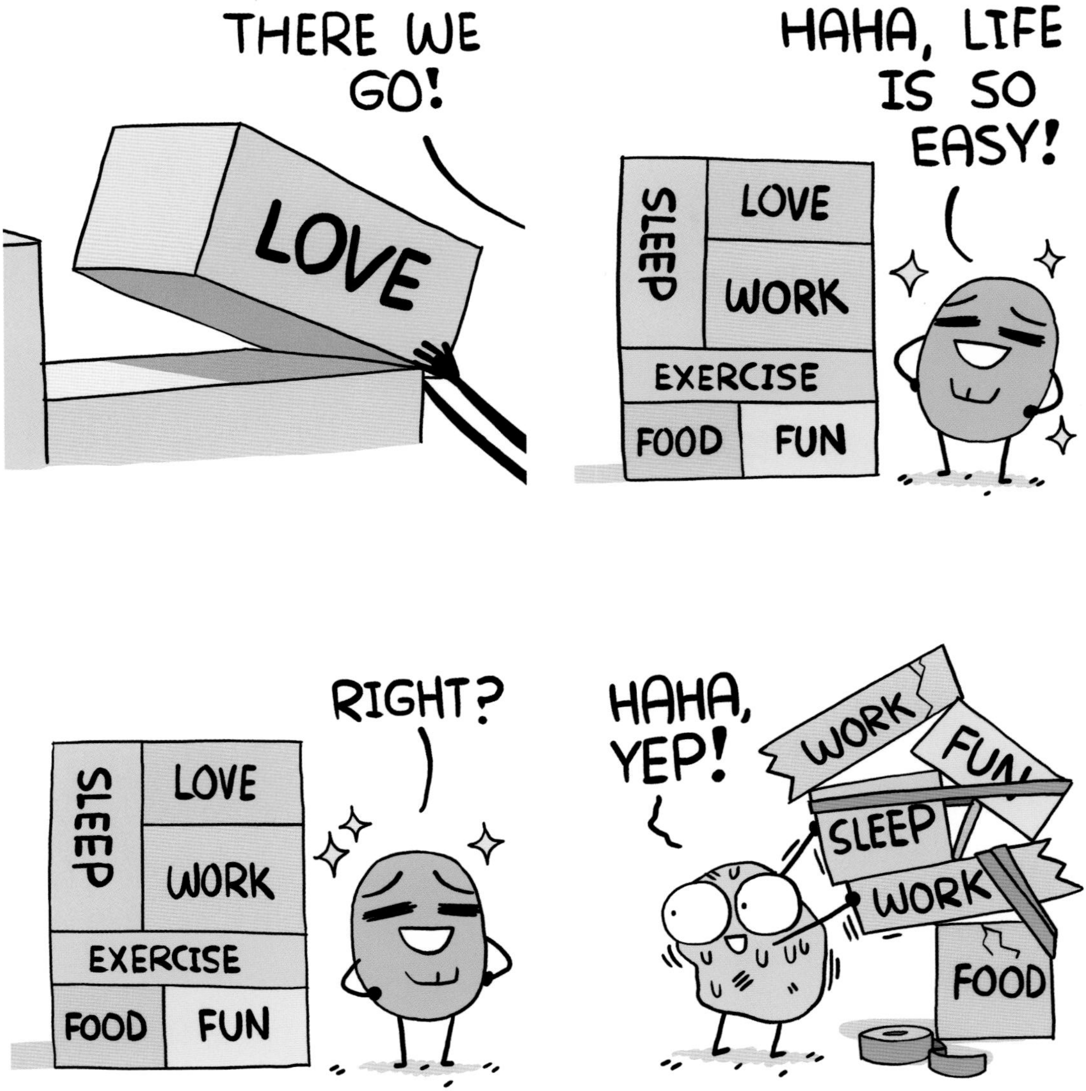
THERE WE GO!
LOVE
HAHA, LIFE IS SO EASY!
SLEEP
LOVE
WORK
EXERCISE
FOOD
FUN
RIGHT?
SLEEP
LOVE
WORK
EXERCISE
FOOD
FUN
HAHA, YEP!
WORK
SLEEP
WORK
FOOD

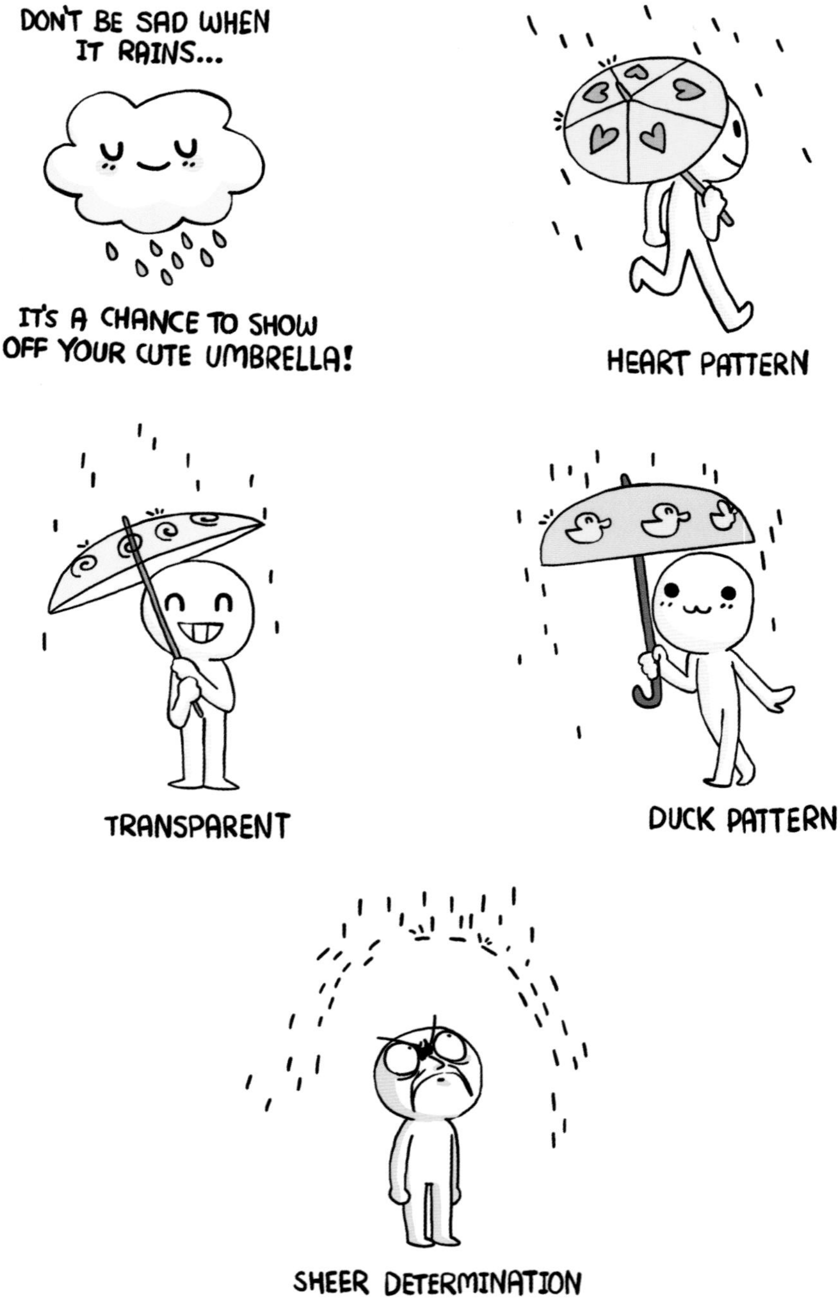
DON'T BE SAD WHEN IT RAINS...
IT'S A CHANCE TO SHOW OFF YOUR CUTE UMBRELLA!
HEART PATTERN
TRANSPARENT
DUCK PATTERN
SHEER DETERMINATION

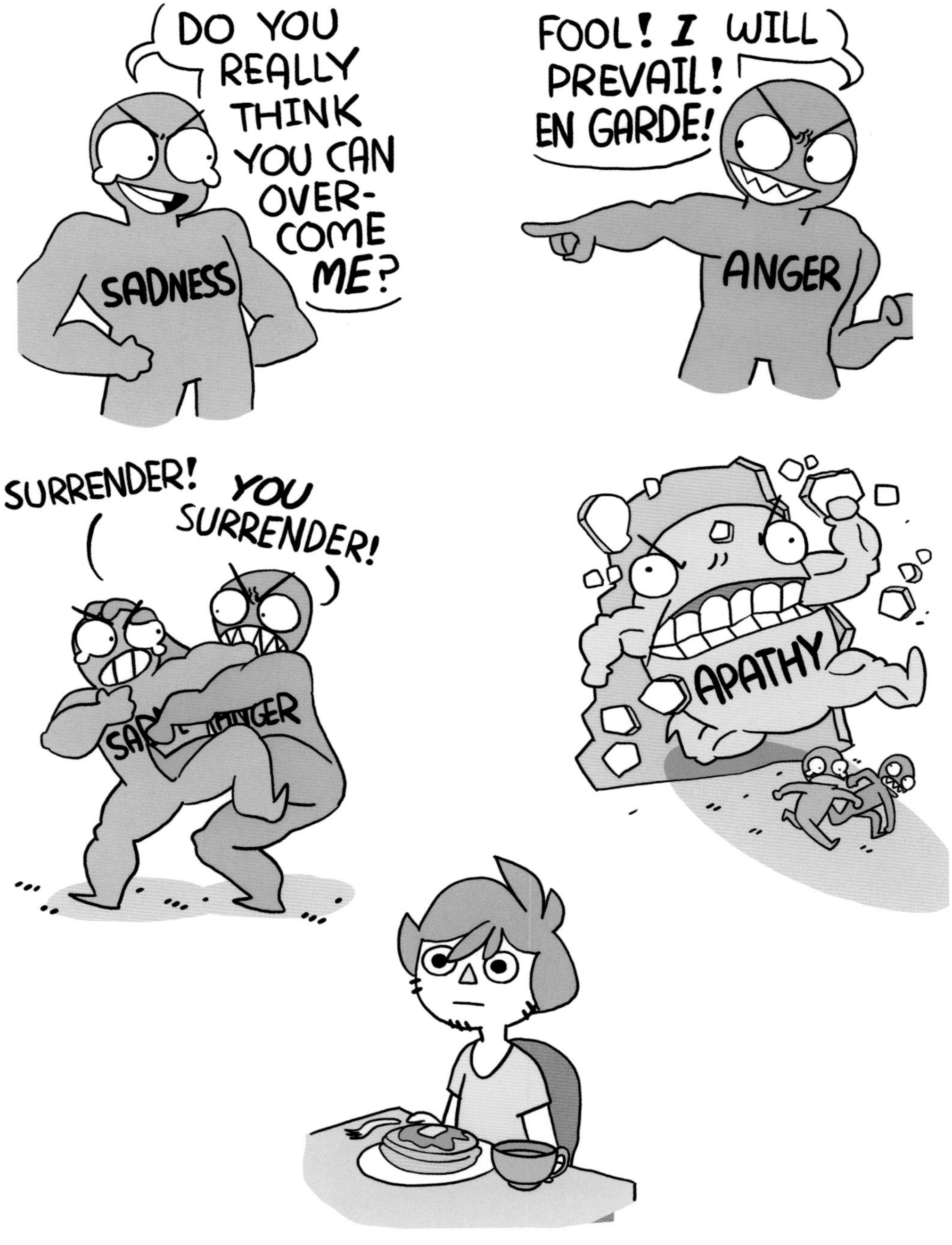
DO YOU REALLY THINK YOU CAN OVER-COME ME?
SADNESS
FOOL! I WILL PREVAIL! EN GARDE!
ANGER
SURRENDER!
YOU SURRENDER!
APATHY

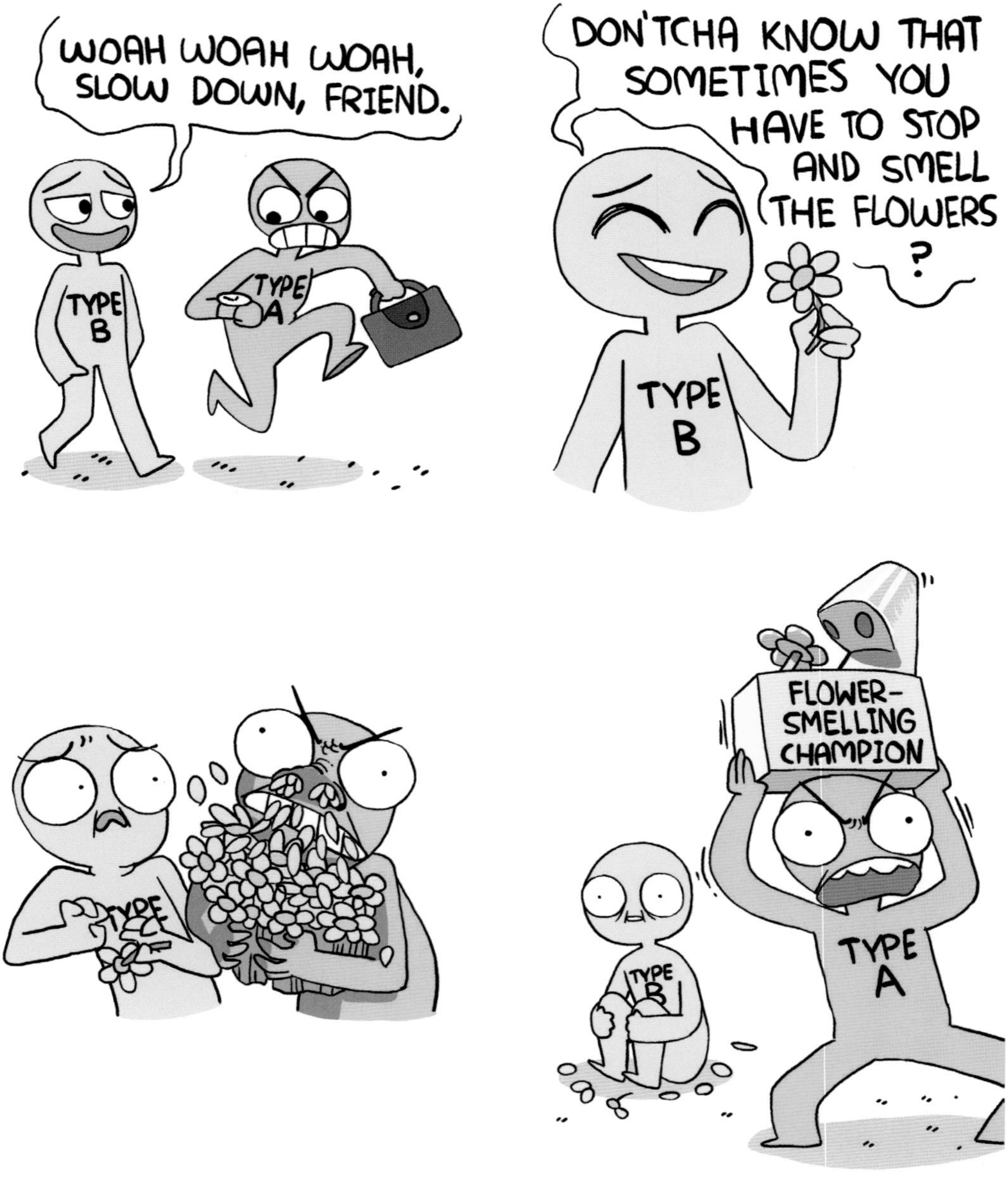

WOAH WOAH WOAH, SLOW DOWN, FRIEND.
TYPE B
TYPE A
DON'TCHA KNOW THAT SOMETIMES YOU HAVE TO STOP AND SMELL THE FLOWERS ?
TYPE B
FLOWER-SMELLING CHAMPION
TYPE B
TYPE A

WE ALL HAVE TIMES OF NEED.

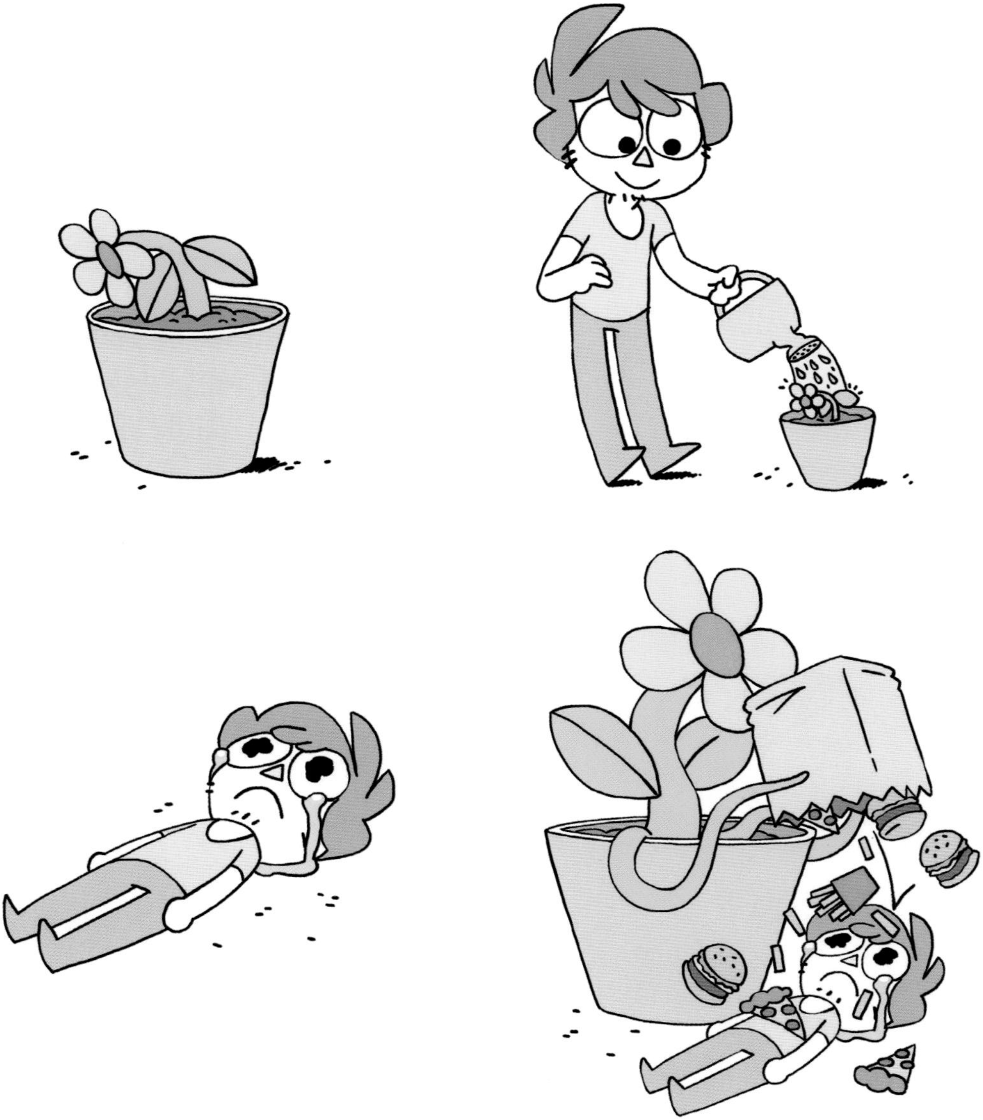

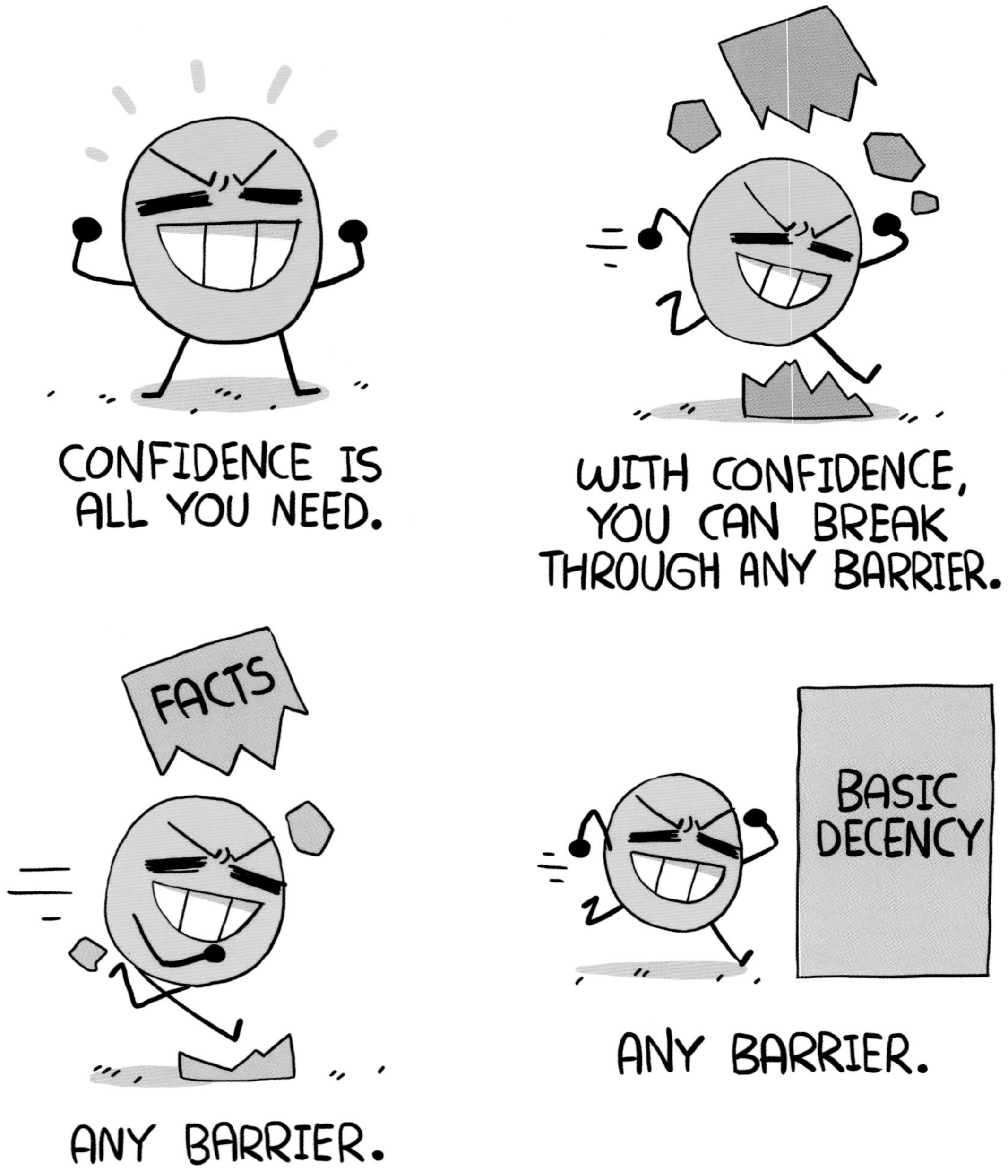
CONFIDENCE IS ALL YOU NEED.
WITH CONFIDENCE, YOU CAN BREAK THROUGH ANY BARRIER.
FACTS
ANY BARRIER.
BASIC DECENCY
ANY BARRIER.

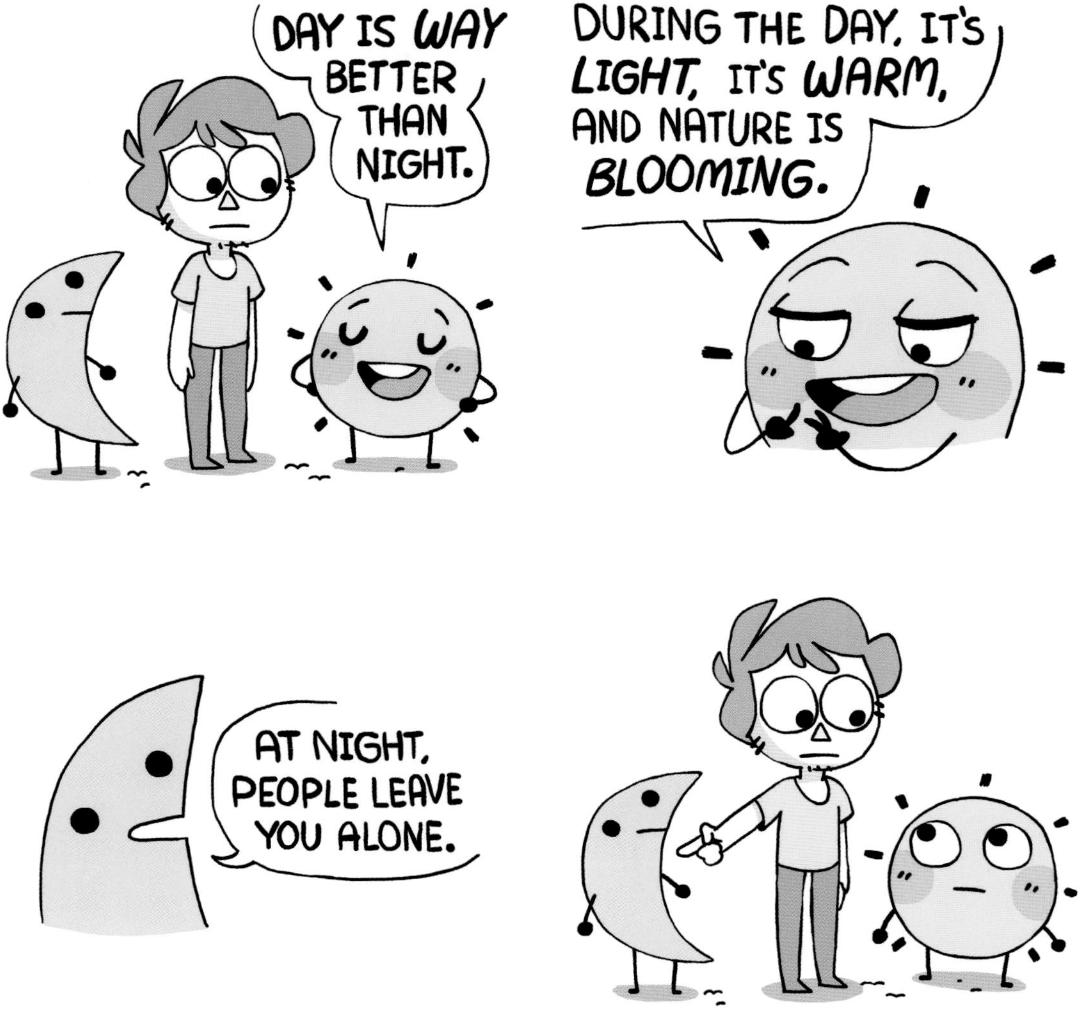
DAY IS WAY BETTER THAN NIGHT.
DURING THE DAY, IT'S LIGHT, IT'S WARM, AND NATURE IS BLOOMING.
AT NIGHT, PEOPLE LEAVE YOU ALONE.

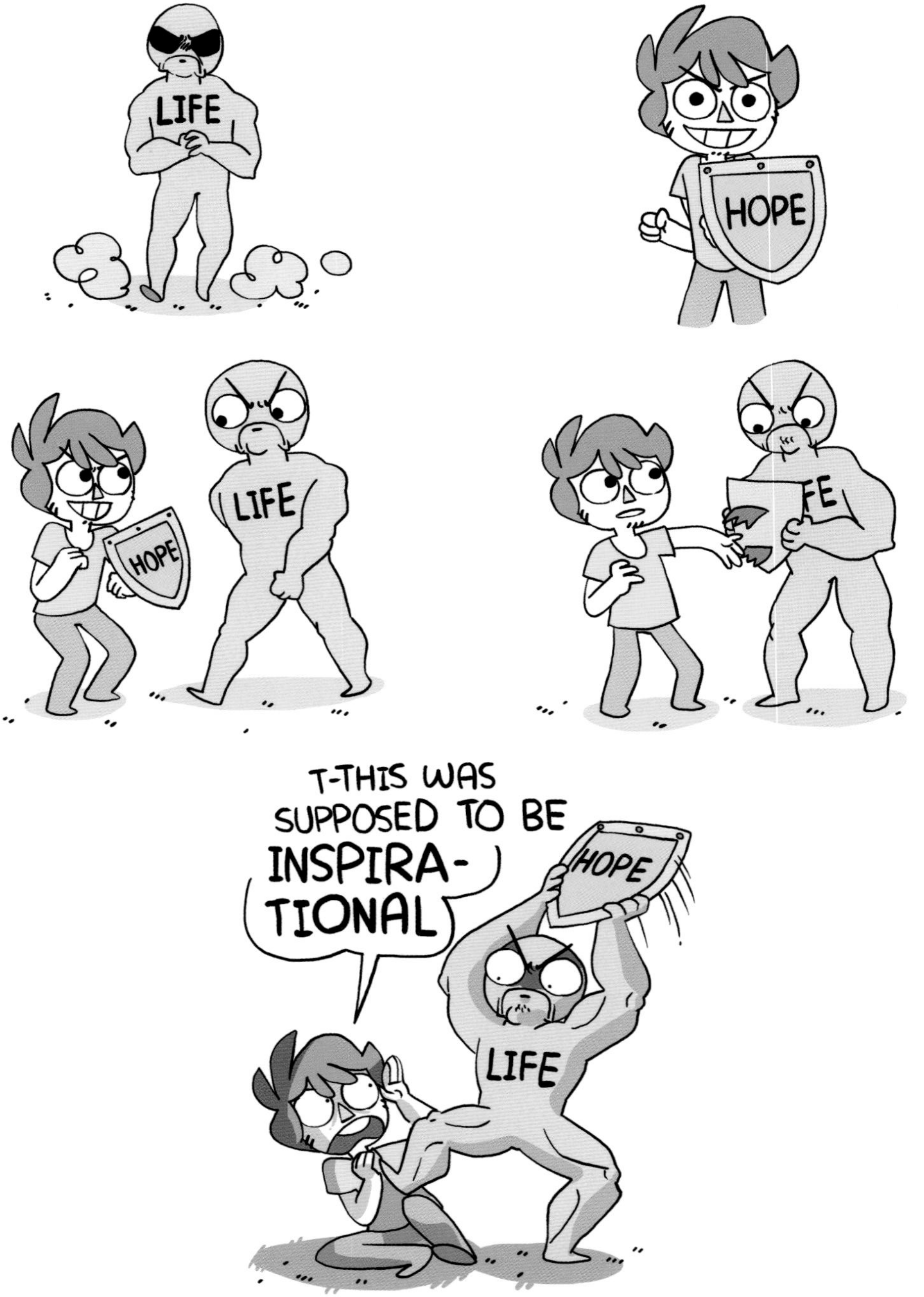
LIFE
HOPE
HOPE
LIFE
FE
T-THIS WAS SUPPOSED TO BE INSPIRA-TIONAL
HOPE
LIFE

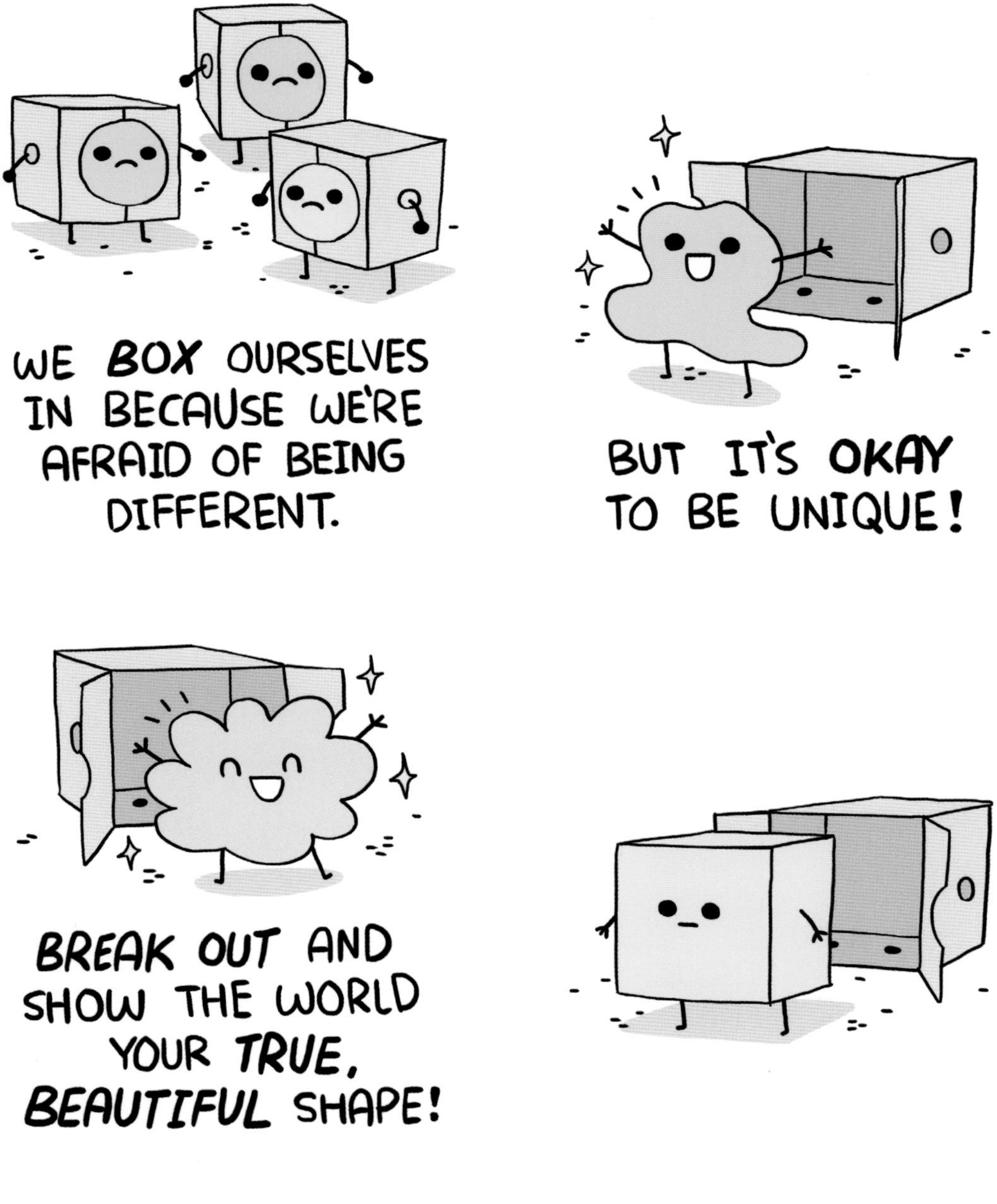
WE BOX OURSELVES IN BECAUSE WE'RE AFRAID OF BEING DIFFERENT.
BUT IT'S OKAY TO BE UNIQUE!
BREAK OUT AND SHOW THE WORLD YOUR TRUE, BEAUTIFUL SHAPE!

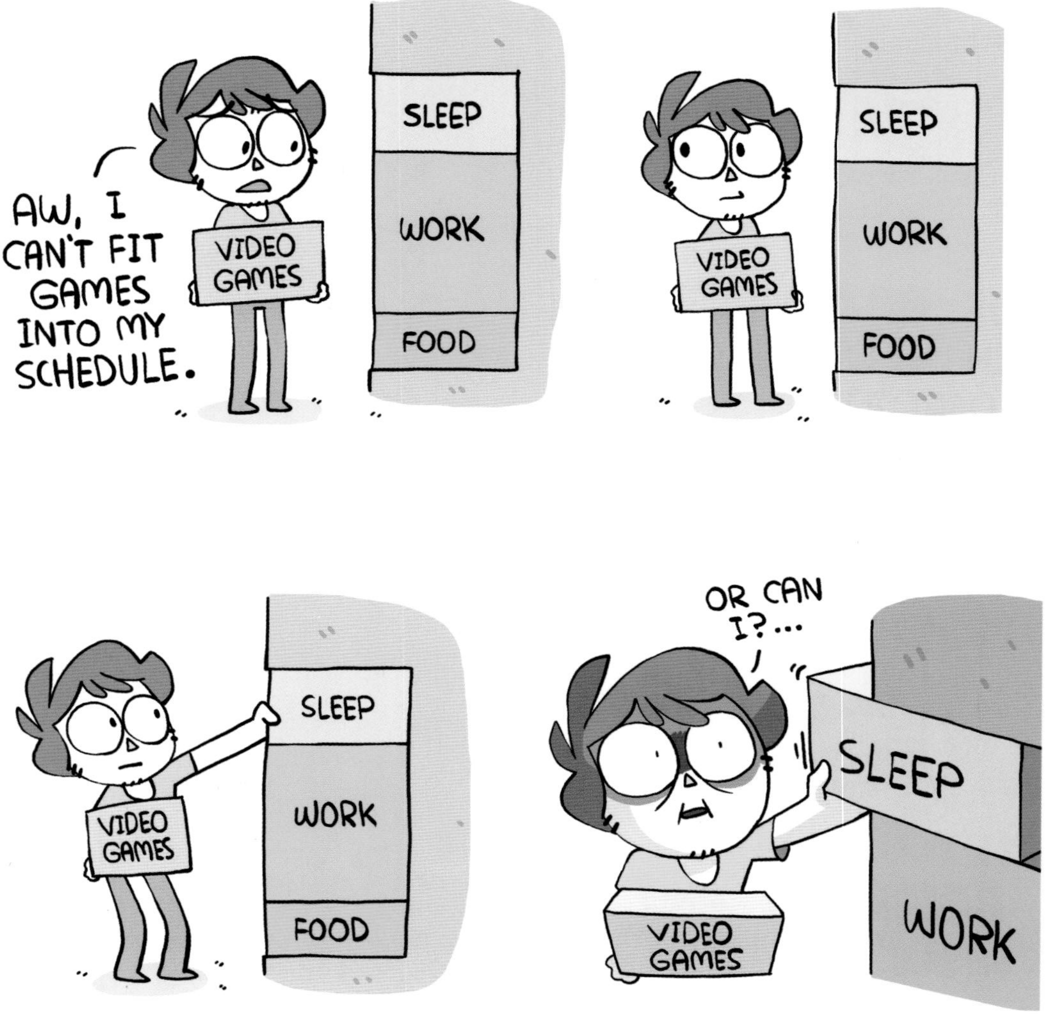
AW, I CAN'T FIT GAMES INTO MY SCHEDULE.
VIDEO GAMES
SLEEP
WORK
FOOD
VIDEO GAMES
SLEEP
WORK
FOOD
VIDEO GAMES
SLEEP
WORK
FOOD
OR CAN I?...
VIDEO GAMES
SLEEP
WORK

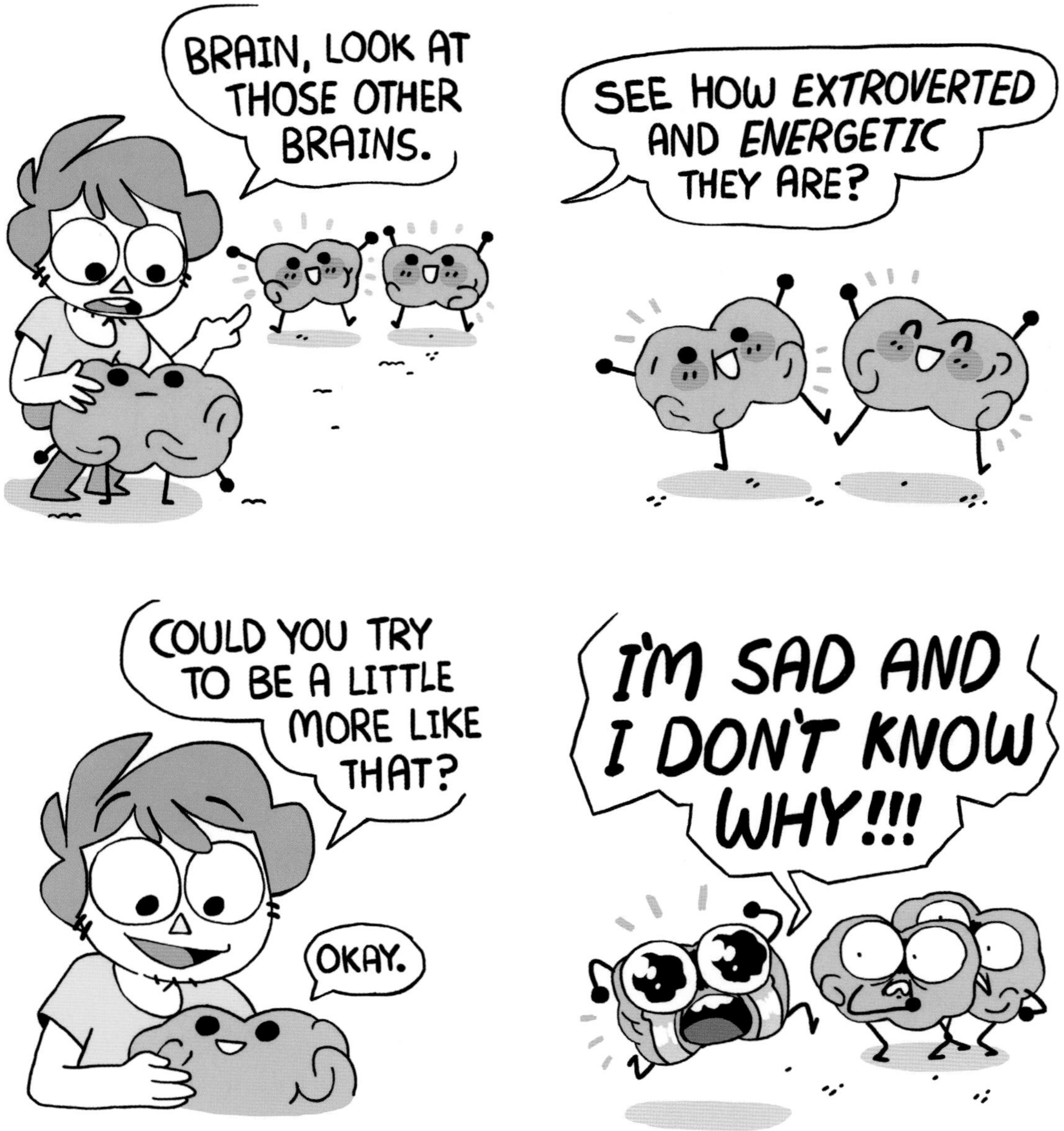
BRAIN, LOOK AT THOSE OTHER BRAINS.
SEE HOW EXTROVERTED AND ENERGETIC THEY ARE?
COULD YOU TRY TO BE A LITTLE MORE LIKE THAT?
OKAY.
I'M SAD AND I DON'T KNOW WHY!!!

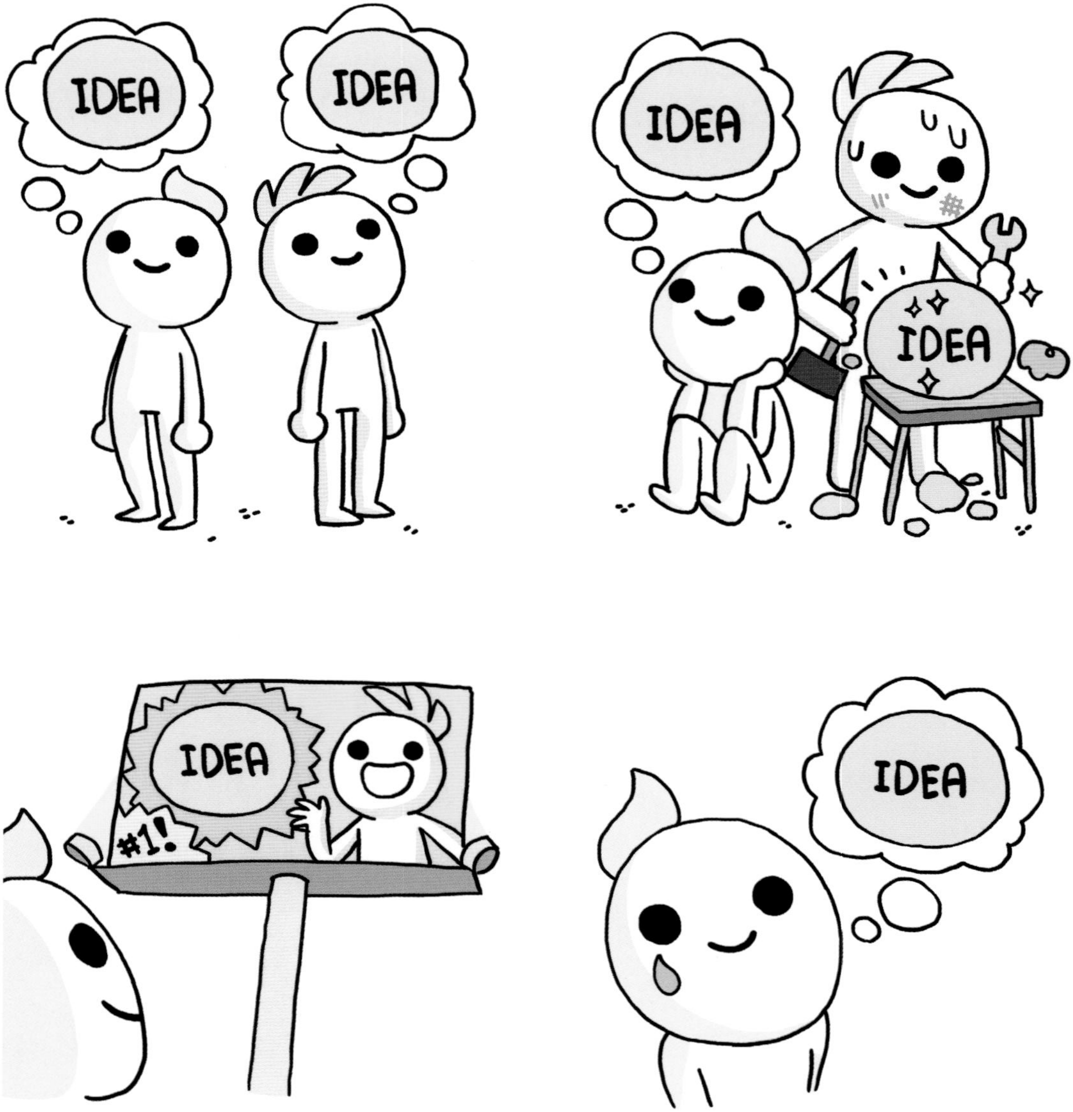

IDEA
IDEA
IDEA
IDEA
IDEA
#1!
IDEA

 PEOPLE GO THROUGH A LOT OF REJECTION.

LOVE, WORK, SCHOOL — ALL *FULL* OF REJECTION.

WE START LIFE AS A MUSHY, SOFT THING.

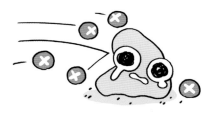

AND THEN, AS WE GET PELTED WITH REJECTION,

WE TRANSFORM INTO A TOUGH, UNFEELING, AND HIGHLY EFFICIENT ROBOT...

PILOTED BY A MUSHY, SOFT THING.

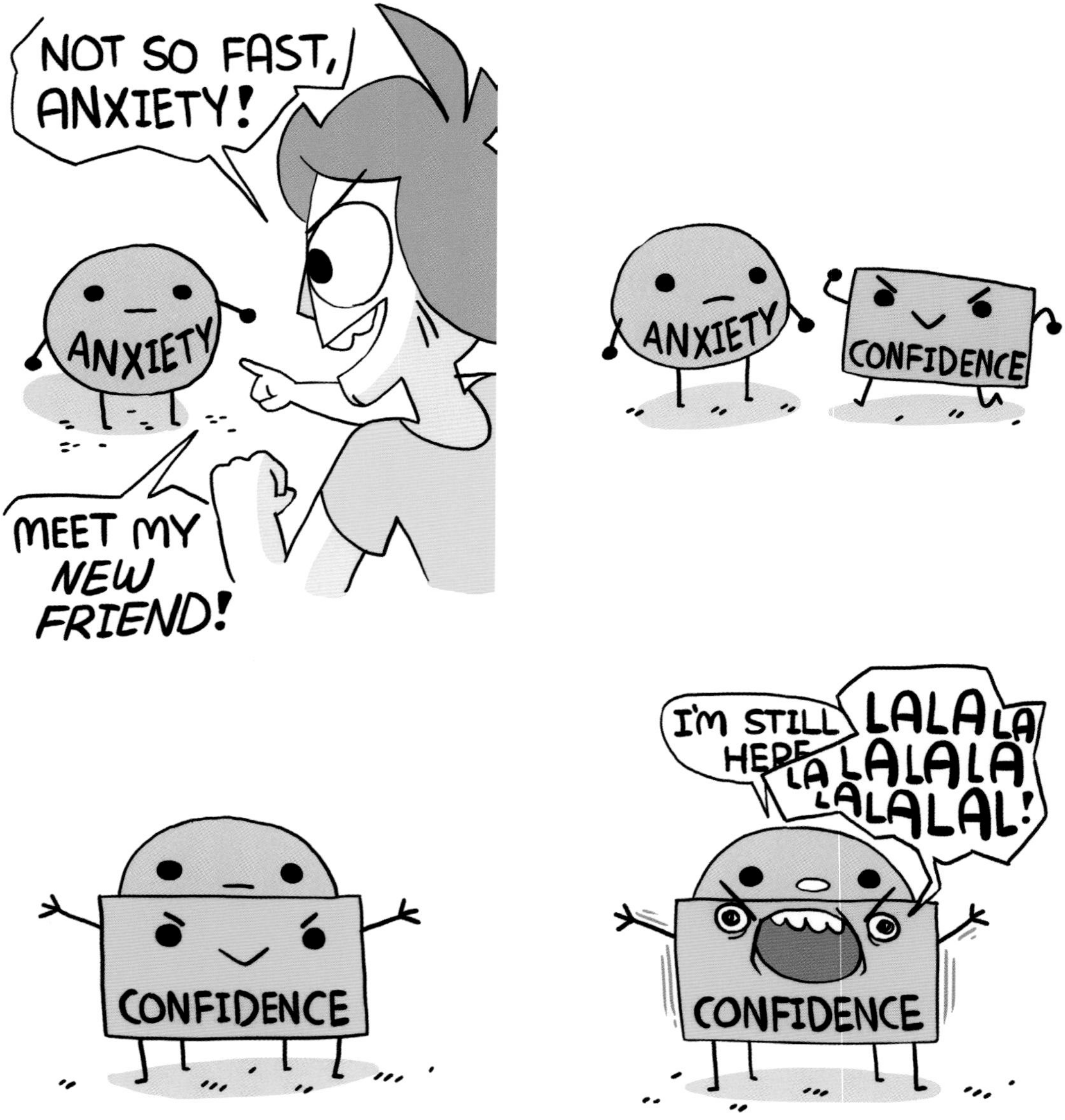
NOT SO FAST, ANXIETY!
ANXIETY
MEET MY NEW FRIEND!
ANXIETY
CONFIDENCE
CONFIDENCE
I'M STILL HER
LALALA LA LALALA LALALAL!
CONFIDENCE

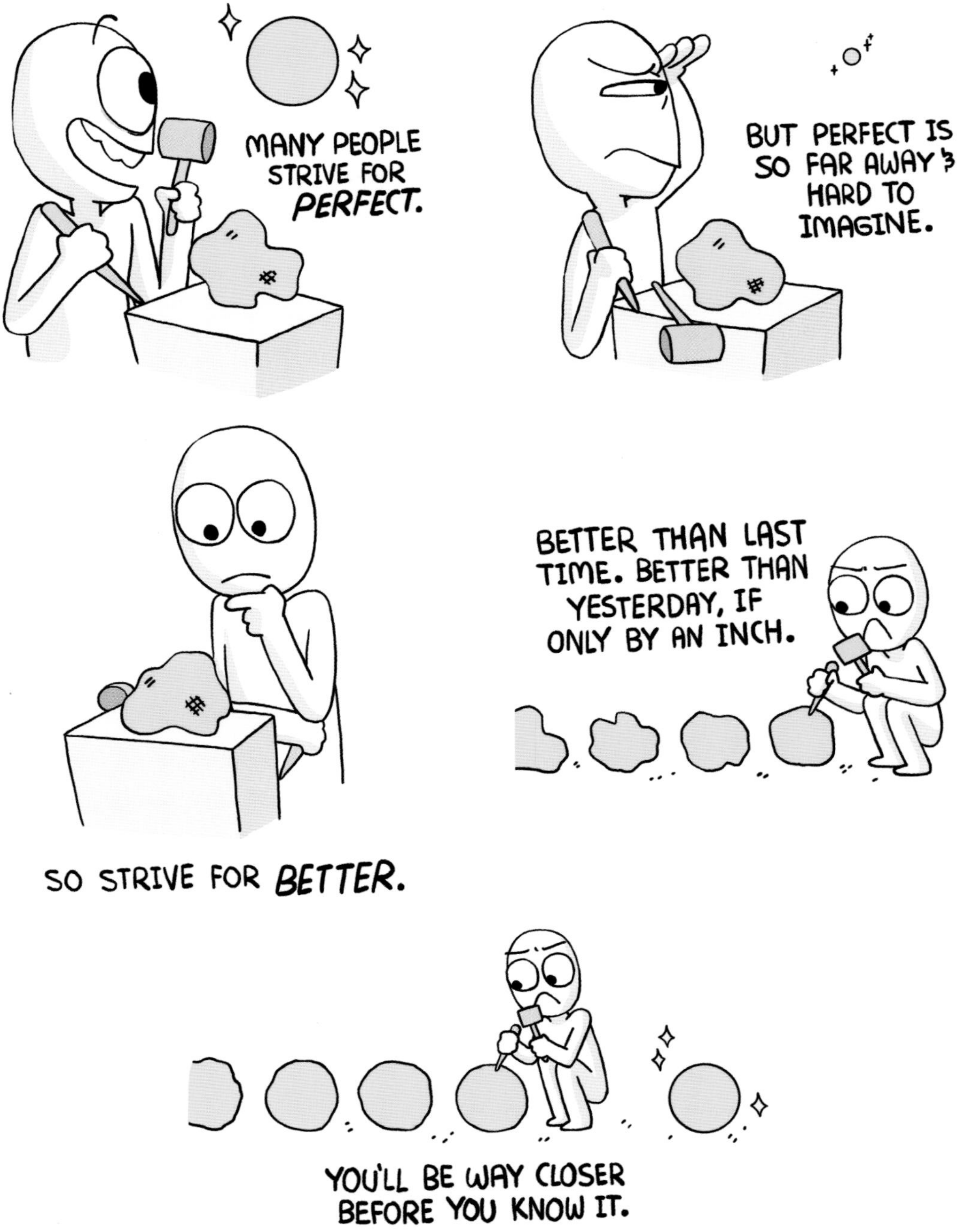
MANY PEOPLE STRIVE FOR PERFECT.
BUT PERFECT IS SO FAR AWAY & HARD TO IMAGINE.
SO STRIVE FOR BETTER.
BETTER THAN LAST TIME. BETTER THAN YESTERDAY, IF ONLY BY AN INCH.
YOU'LL BE WAY CLOSER BEFORE YOU KNOW IT.

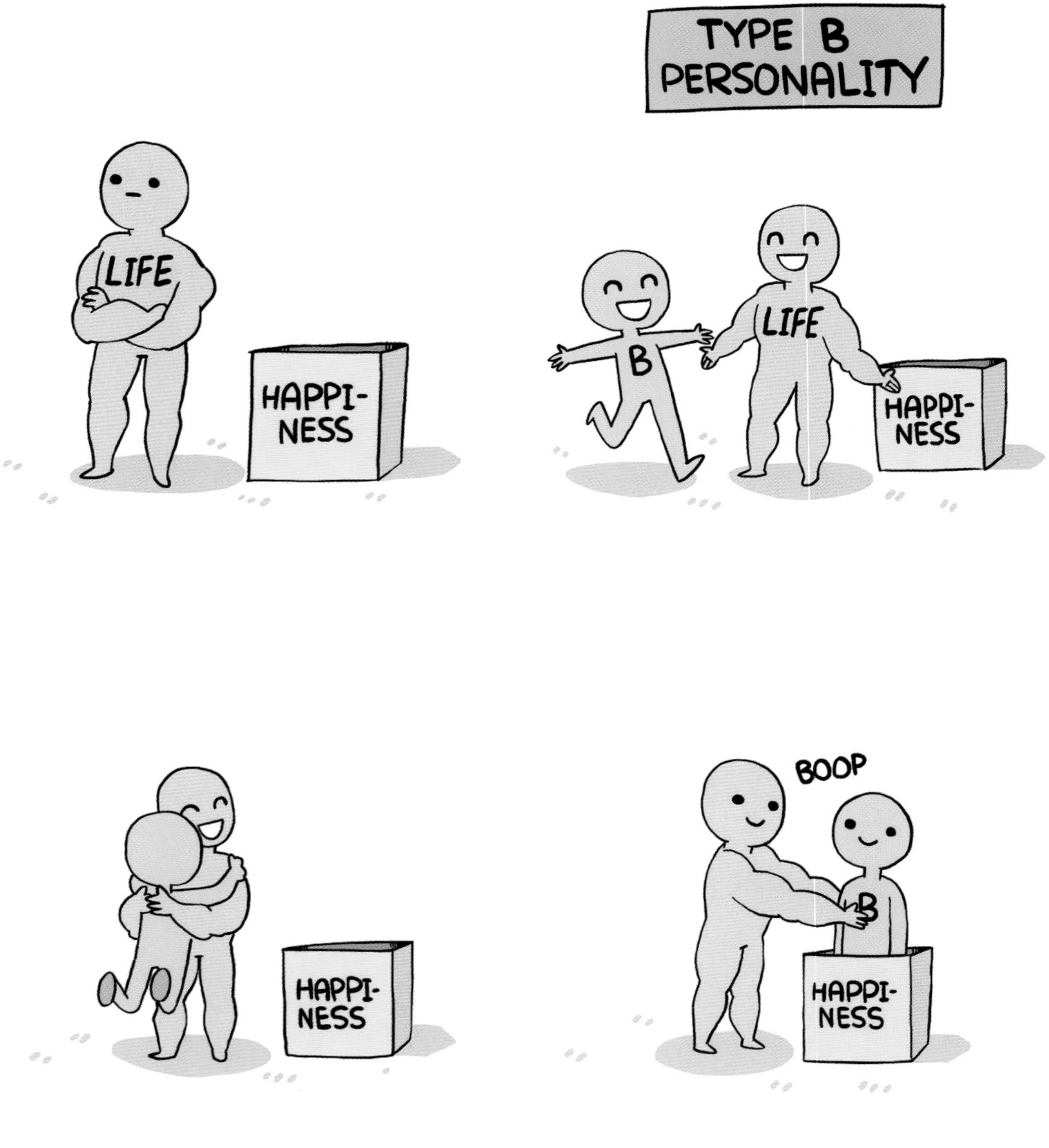
TYPE B PERSONALITY
LIFE
HAPPI-NESS
B
LIFE
HAPPI-NESS
HAPPI-NESS
BOOP
B
HAPPI-NESS

TYPE A PERSONALITY

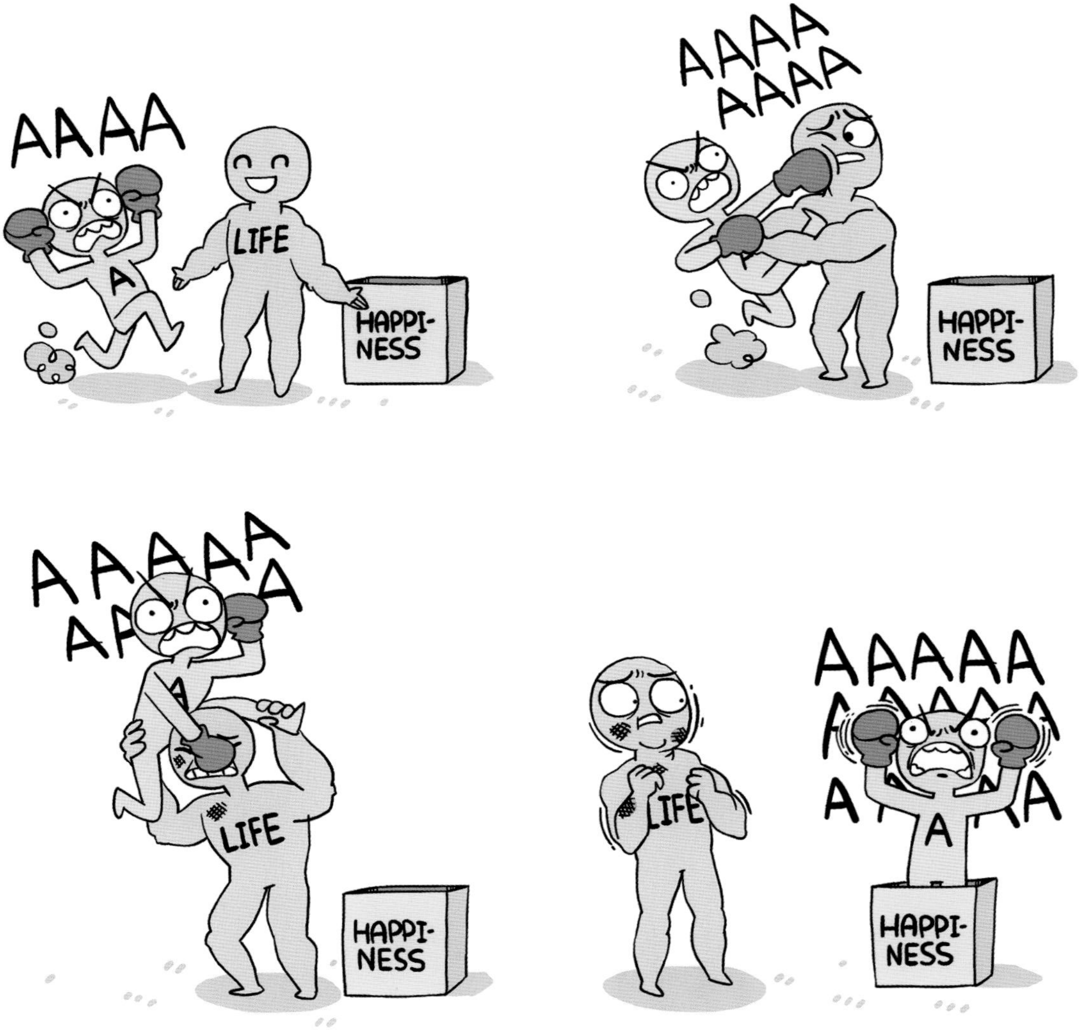

AAAA
A
LIFE
HAPPI-
NESS
AAAA
AAAA
HAPPI-
NESS
LIFE
HAPPI-
NESS
LIFE
AAAAA
A
HAPPI-
NESS

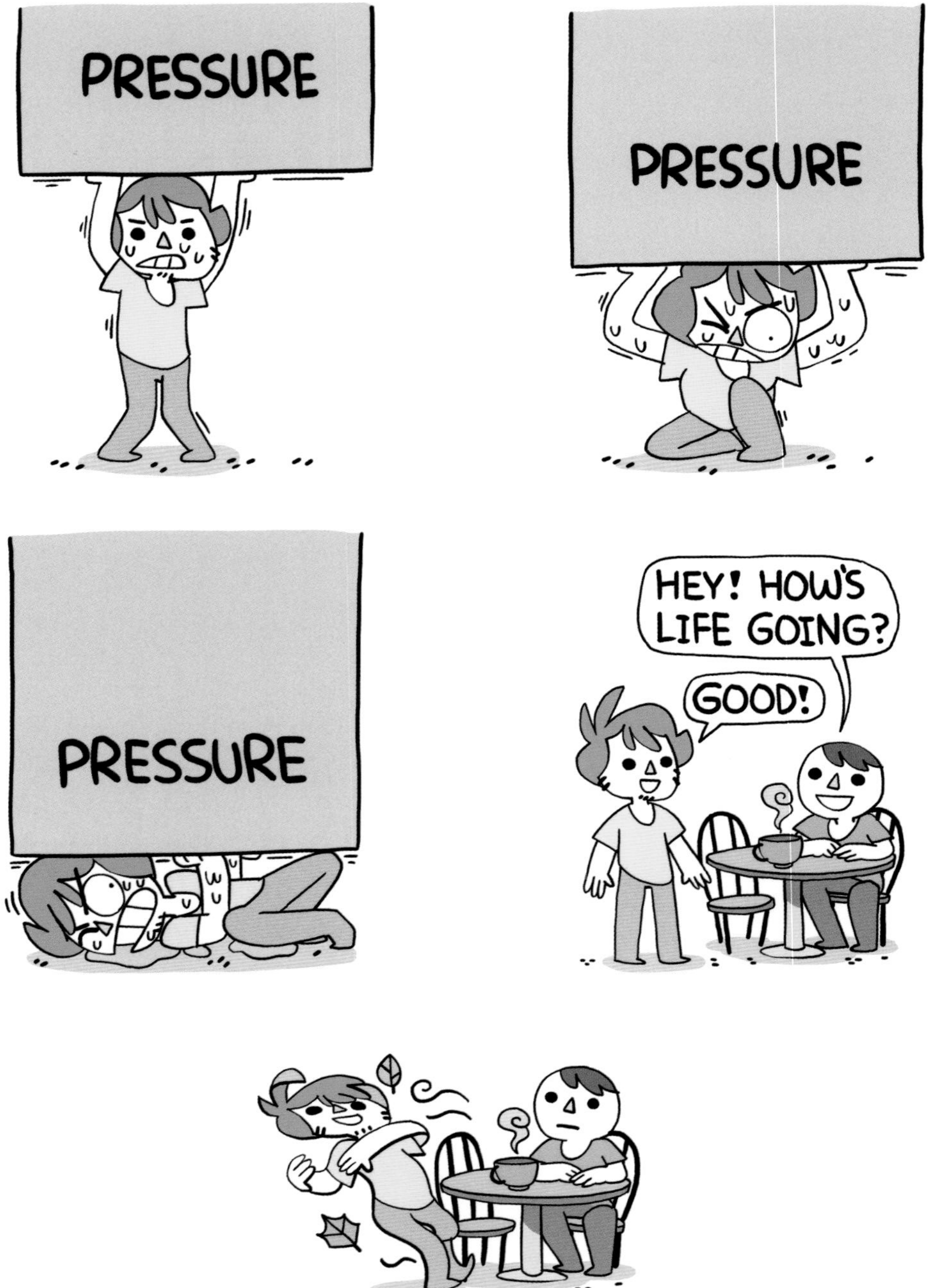
PRESSURE
PRESSURE
PRESSURE
HEY! HOW'S LIFE GOING?
GOOD!

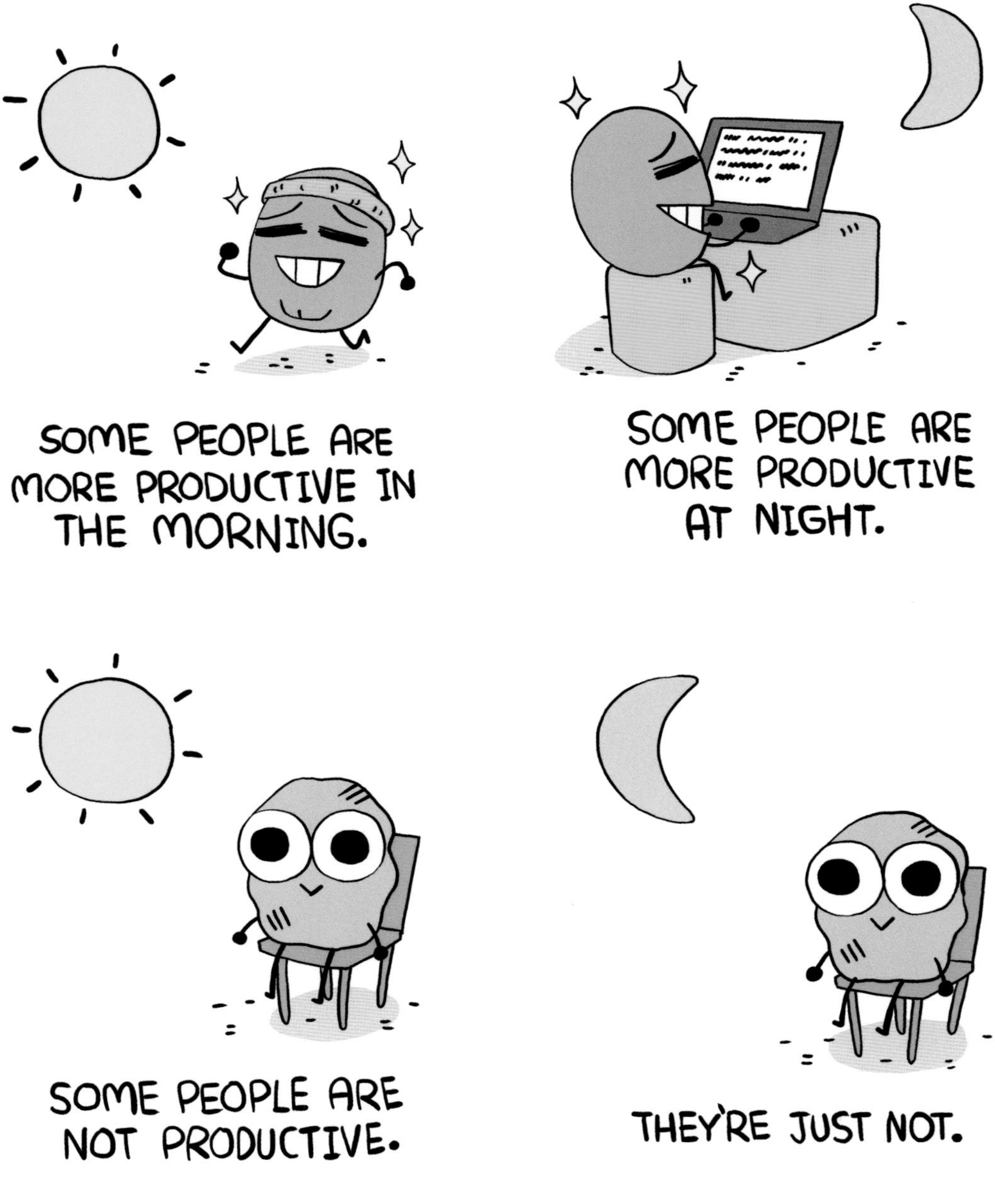
SOME PEOPLE ARE MORE PRODUCTIVE IN THE MORNING.
SOME PEOPLE ARE MORE PRODUCTIVE AT NIGHT.
SOME PEOPLE ARE NOT PRODUCTIVE.
THEY'RE JUST NOT.

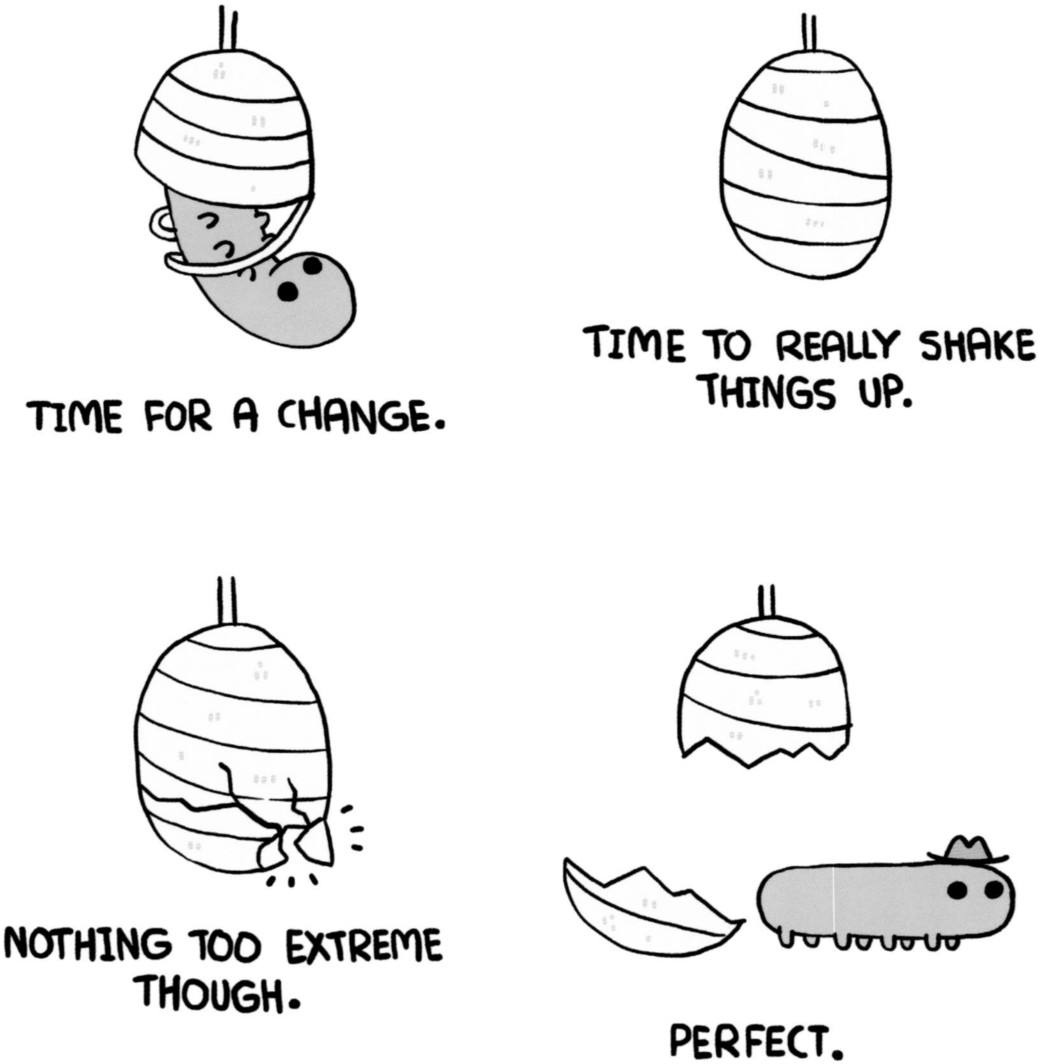
TIME FOR A CHANGE.
TIME TO REALLY SHAKE THINGS UP.
NOTHING TOO EXTREME THOUGH.
PERFECT.

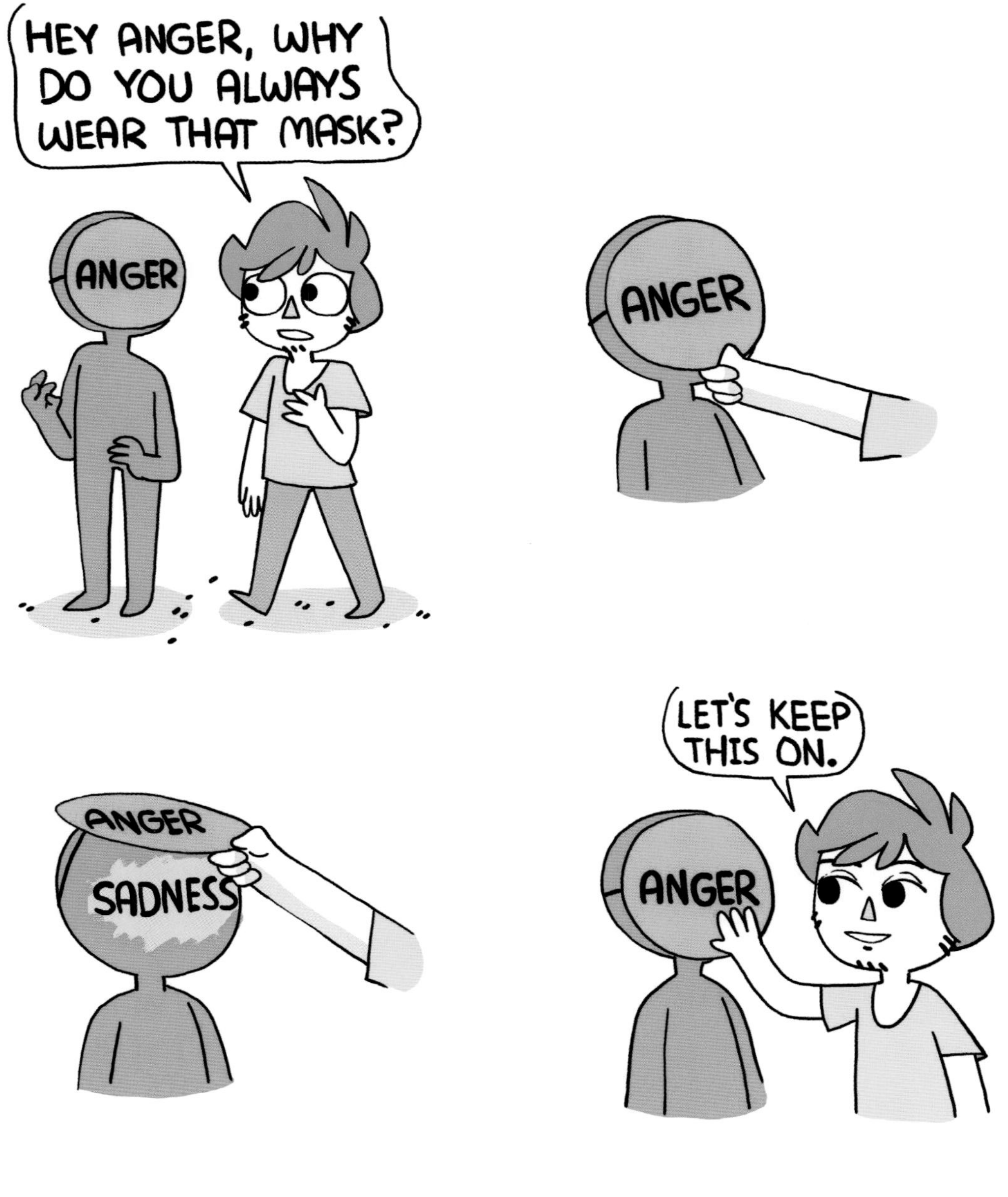
HEY ANGER, WHY DO YOU ALWAYS WEAR THAT MASK?
ANGER
ANGER
ANGER
SADNESS
LET'S KEEP THIS ON.
ANGER

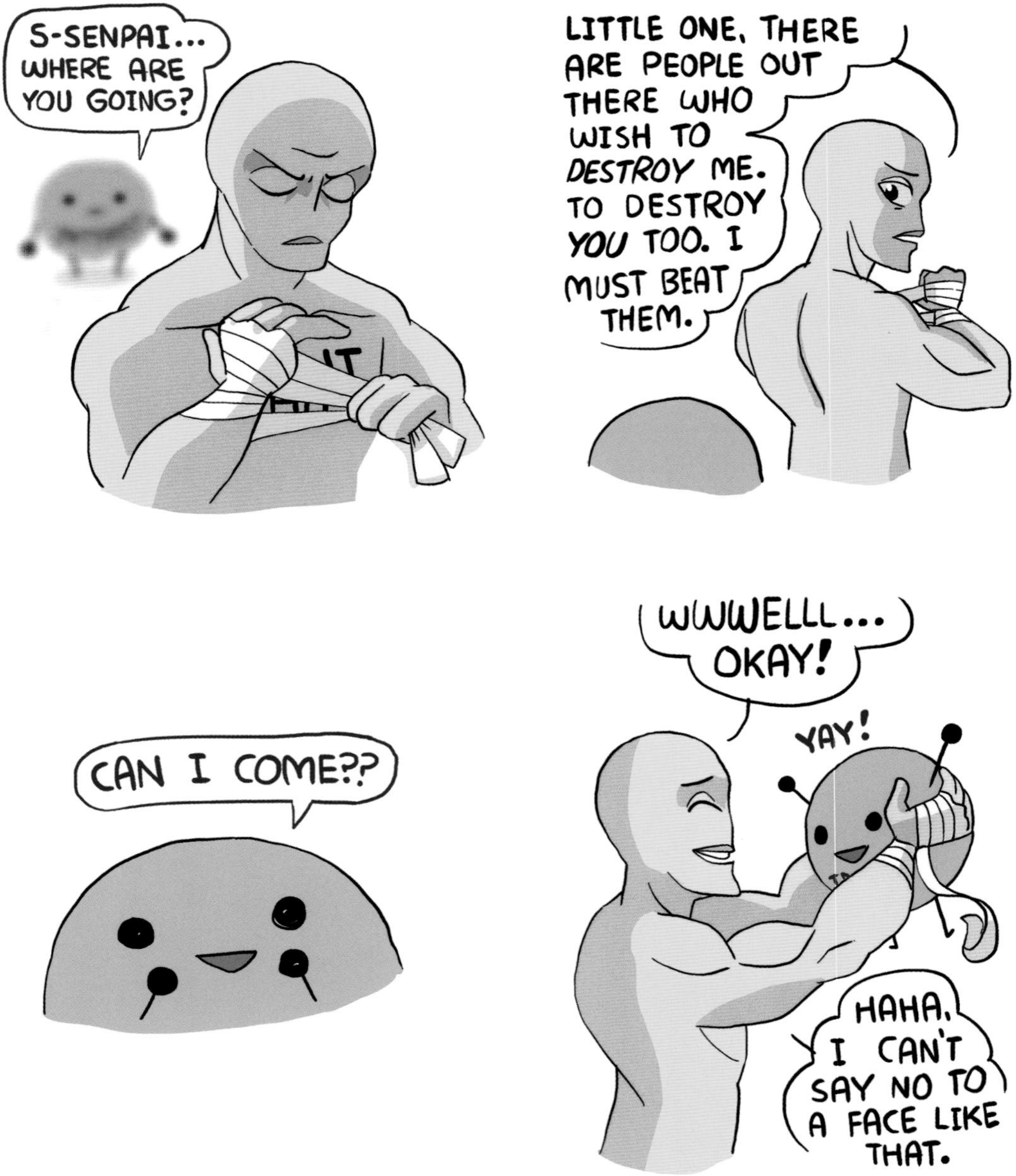
S-SENPAI... WHERE ARE YOU GOING?
LITTLE ONE, THERE ARE PEOPLE OUT THERE WHO WISH TO *DESTROY* ME. TO DESTROY *YOU* TOO. I MUST BEAT THEM.
CAN I COME??
WWWELLL... OKAY!
YAY!
HAHA, I CAN'T SAY NO TO A FACE LIKE THAT.

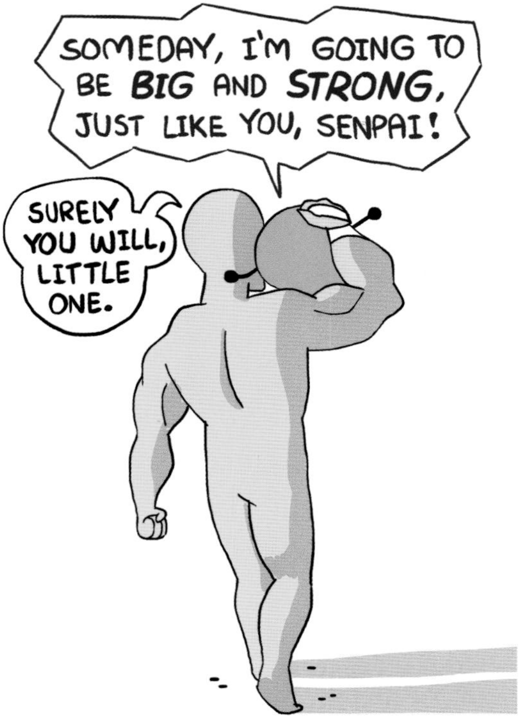
SOMEDAY, I'M GOING TO BE **BIG** AND **STRONG**, JUST LIKE YOU, SENPAI!
SURELY YOU WILL, LITTLE ONE.

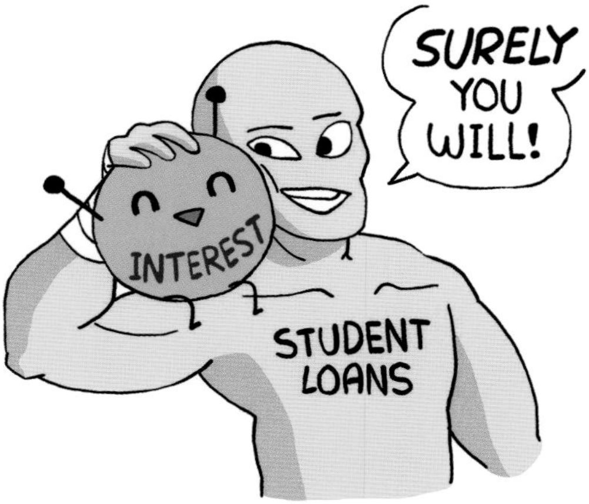
SURELY YOU WILL!
INTEREST
STUDENT LOANS

WAYS to GET ENERGY

SLEEP, IF YOU WANT TO LIVE CALMLY.

TEA, IF YOU WANT TO LIVE MODERATELY.

COFFEE, IF YOU WANT TO LIVE DANGEROUSLY.

ENERGY DRINKS, IF YOU WANT TO DIE.

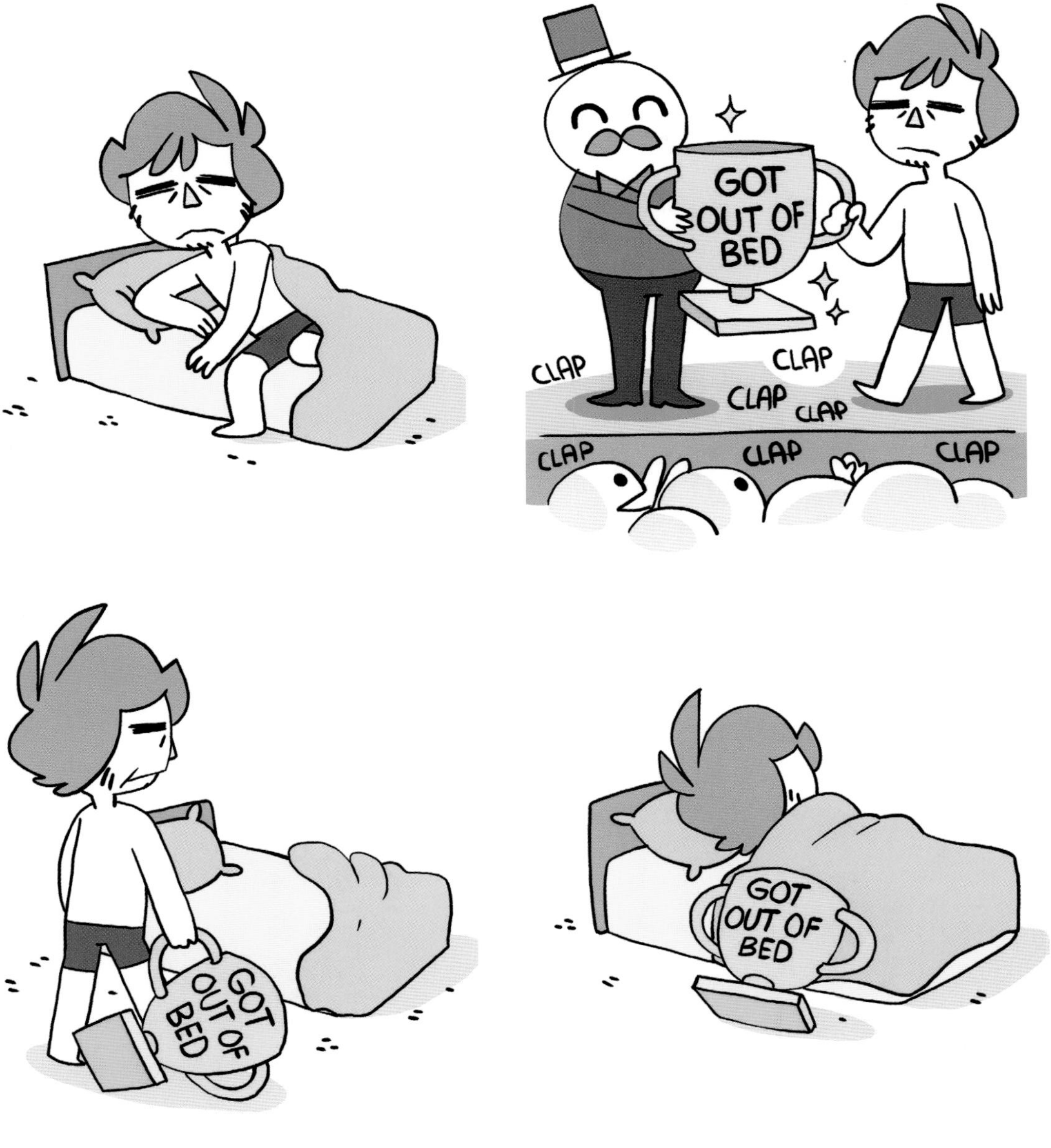
GOT OUT OF BED
CLAP
CLAP
CLAP
CLAP
CLAP
CLAP
CLAP
GOT OUT OF BED
GOT OUT OF BED

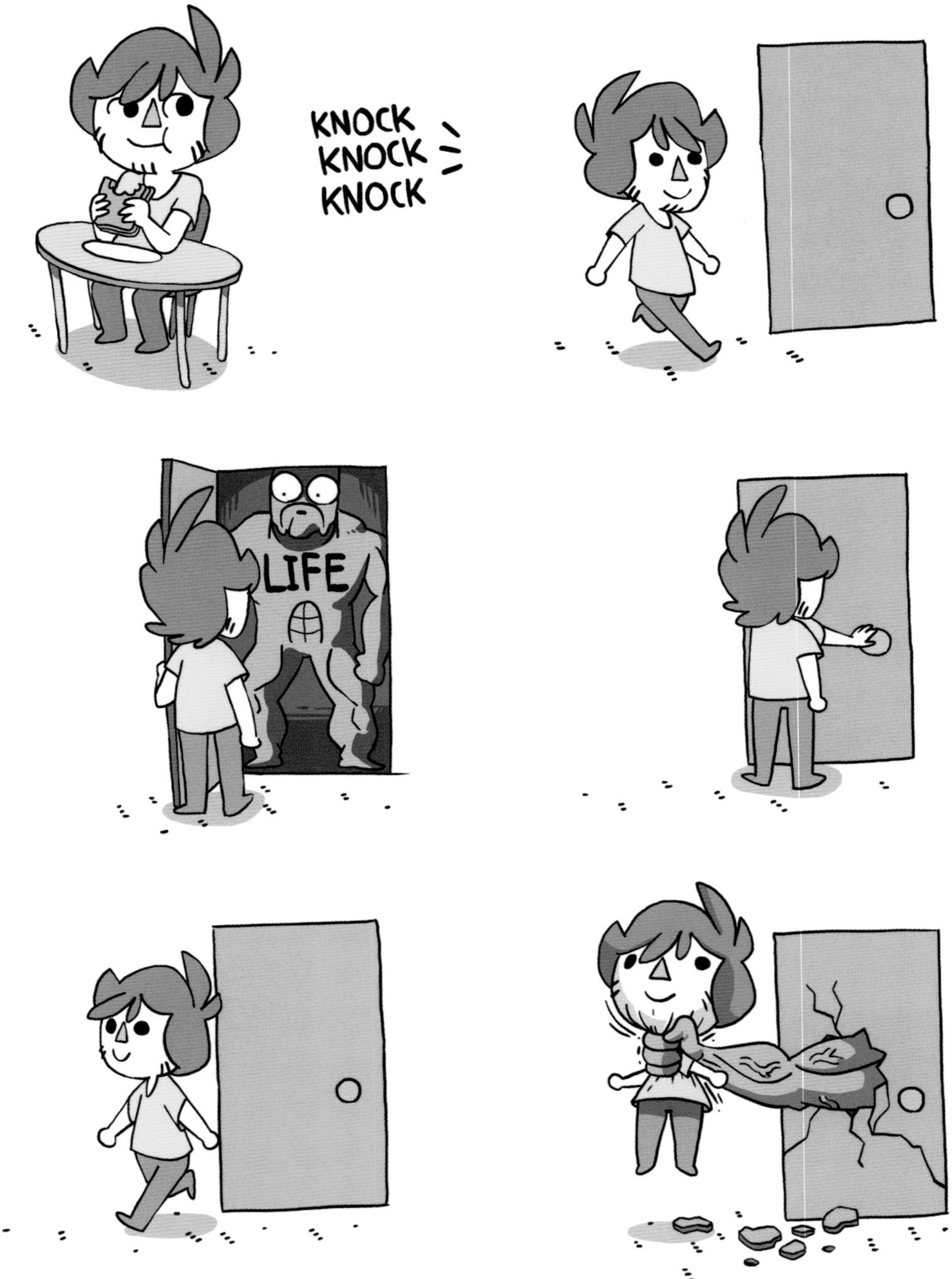
KNOCK
KNOCK
KNOCK
LIFE

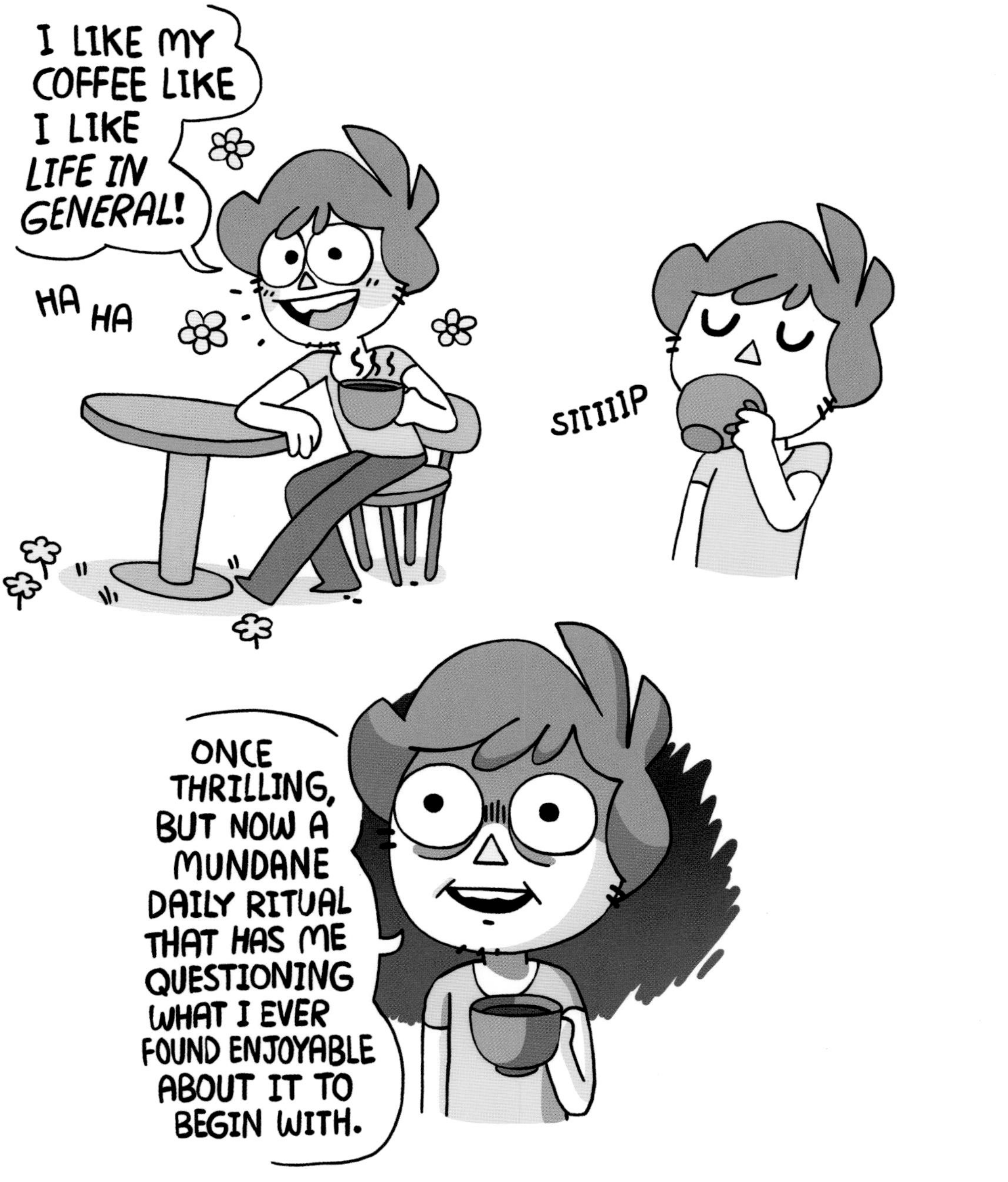
I LIKE MY COFFEE LIKE I LIKE LIFE IN GENERAL!
HA HA
SIIIIIP
ONCE THRILLING, BUT NOW A MUNDANE DAILY RITUAL THAT HAS ME QUESTIONING WHAT I EVER FOUND ENJOYABLE ABOUT IT TO BEGIN WITH.

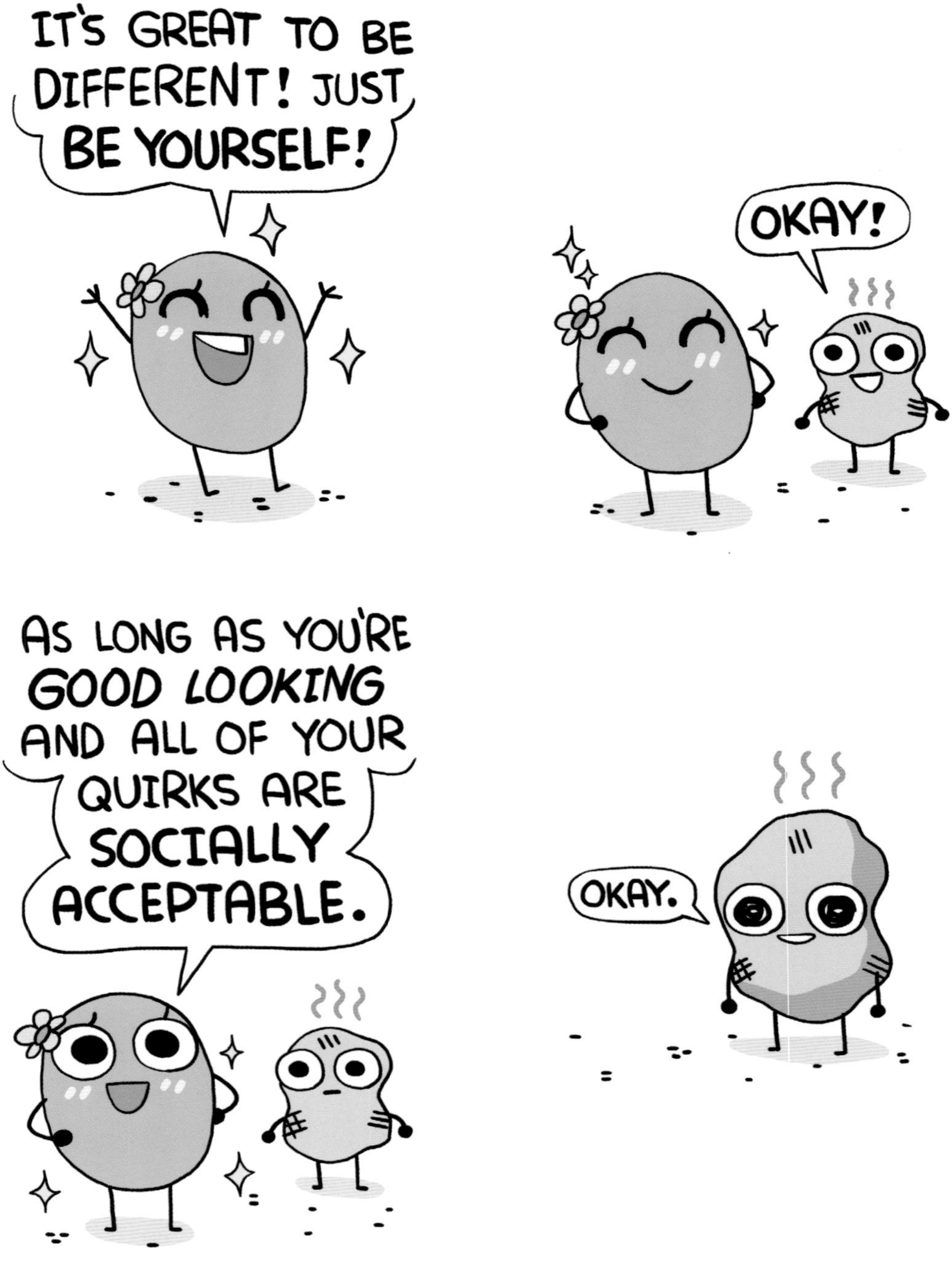
IT'S GREAT TO BE DIFFERENT! JUST BE YOURSELF!
OKAY!
AS LONG AS YOU'RE GOOD LOOKING AND ALL OF YOUR QUIRKS ARE SOCIALLY ACCEPTABLE.
OKAY.

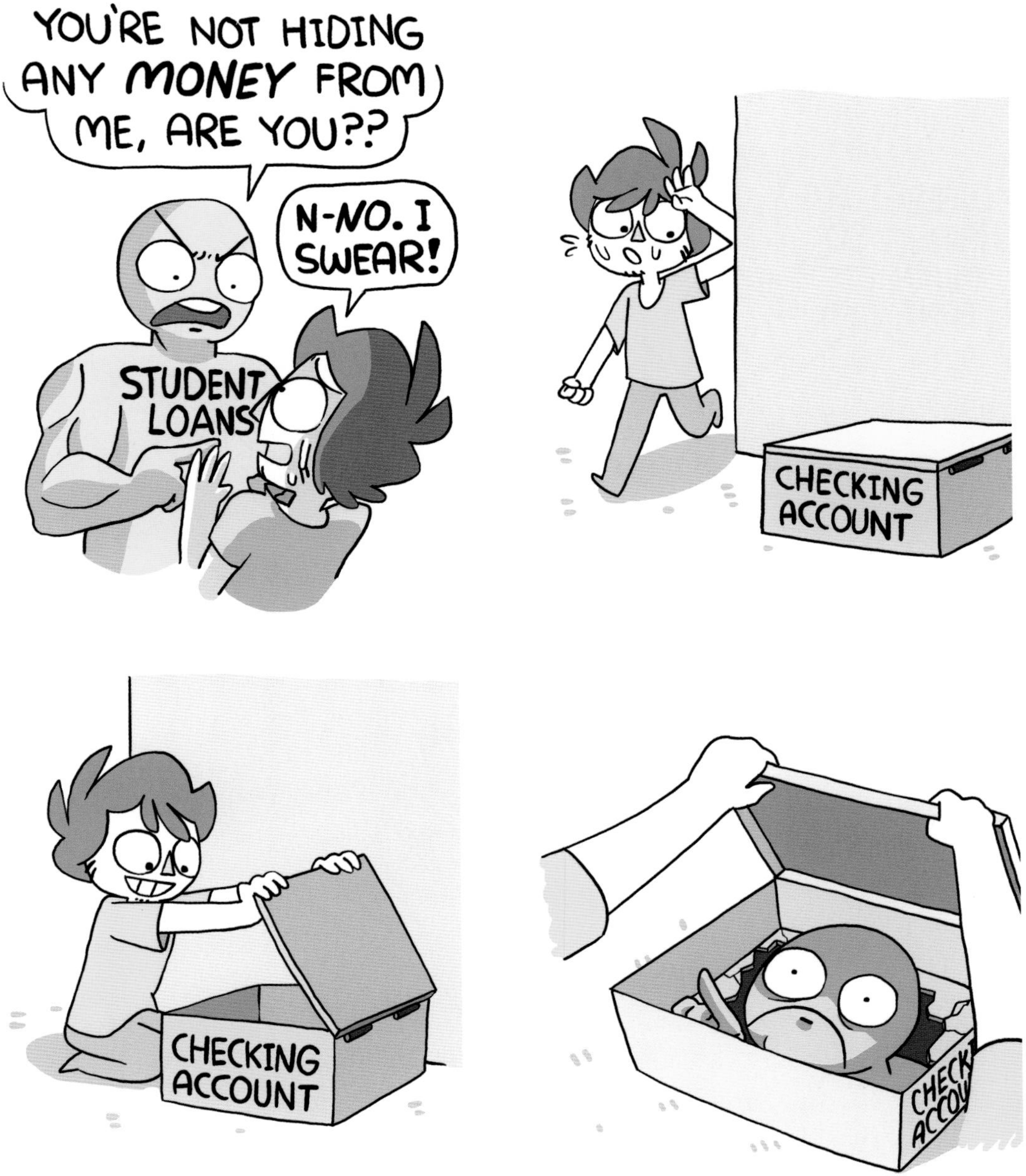
YOU'RE NOT HIDING ANY MONEY FROM ME, ARE YOU??
N-NO. I SWEAR!
STUDENT LOANS
CHECKING ACCOUNT
CHECKING ACCOUNT

TIME FLIES WHEN YOU'RE HAVING FUN.

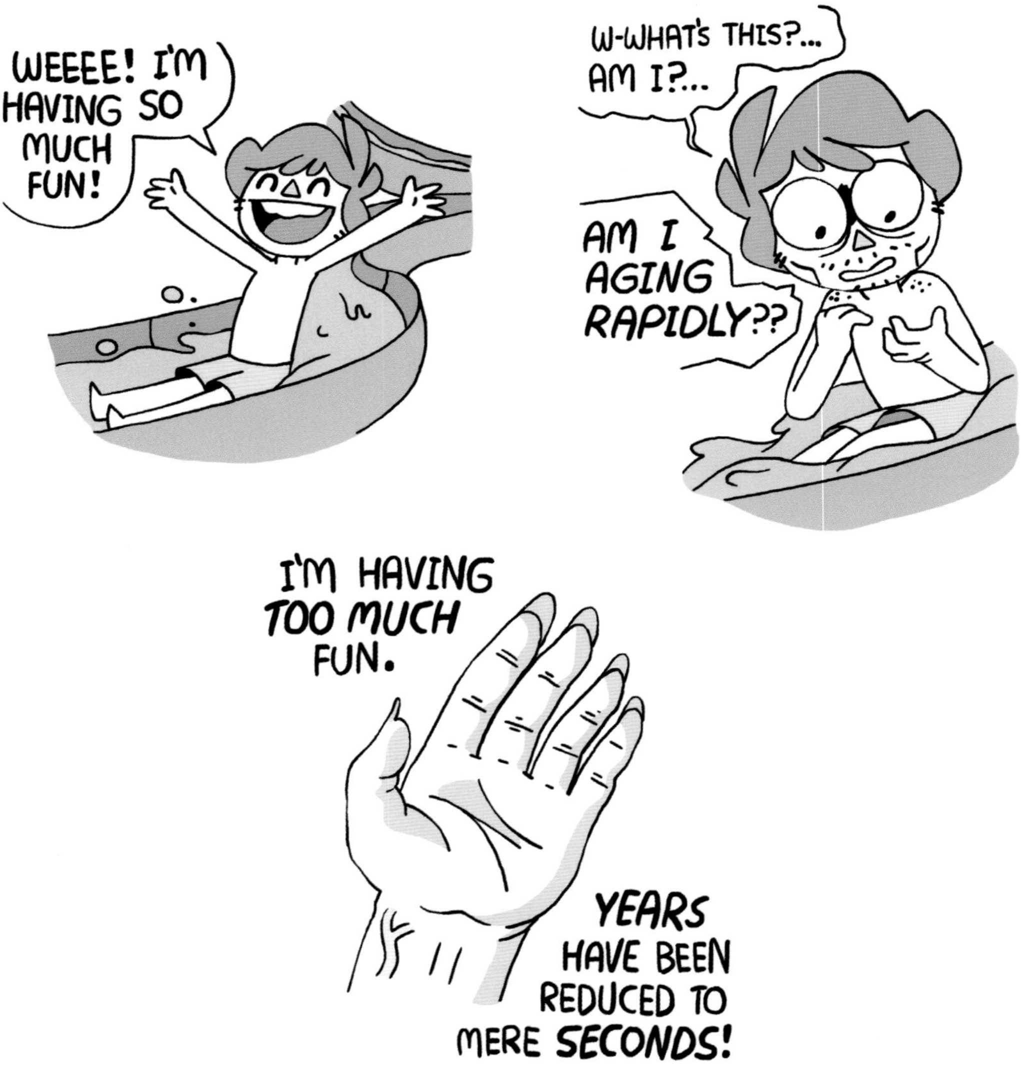

WEEEE! I'M HAVING SO MUCH FUN!
W-WHAT'S THIS?... AM I?...
AM I AGING RAPIDLY??
I'M HAVING TOO MUCH FUN.
YEARS HAVE BEEN REDUCED TO MERE SECONDS!

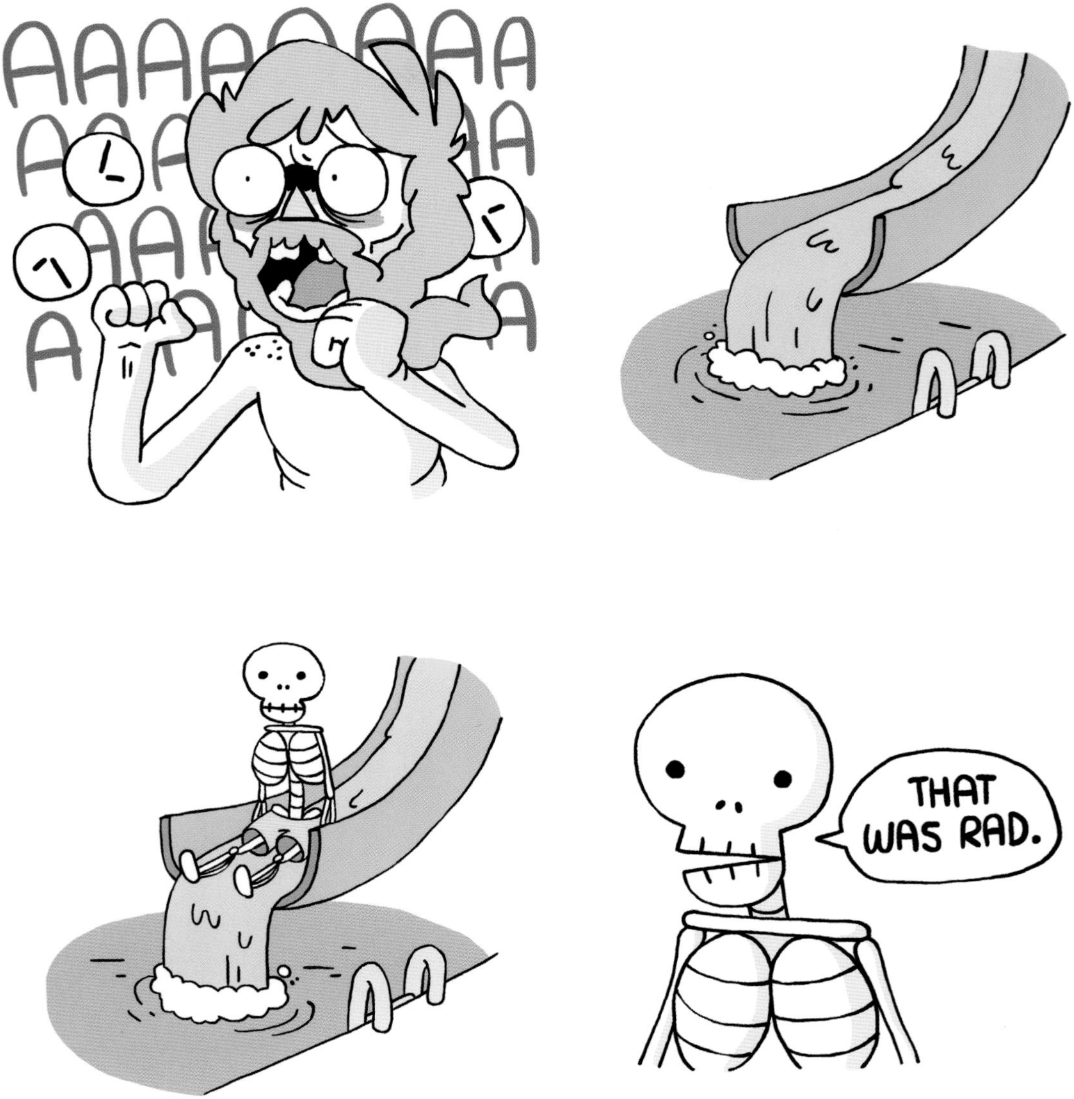
AAAAAAAA
THAT WAS RAD.

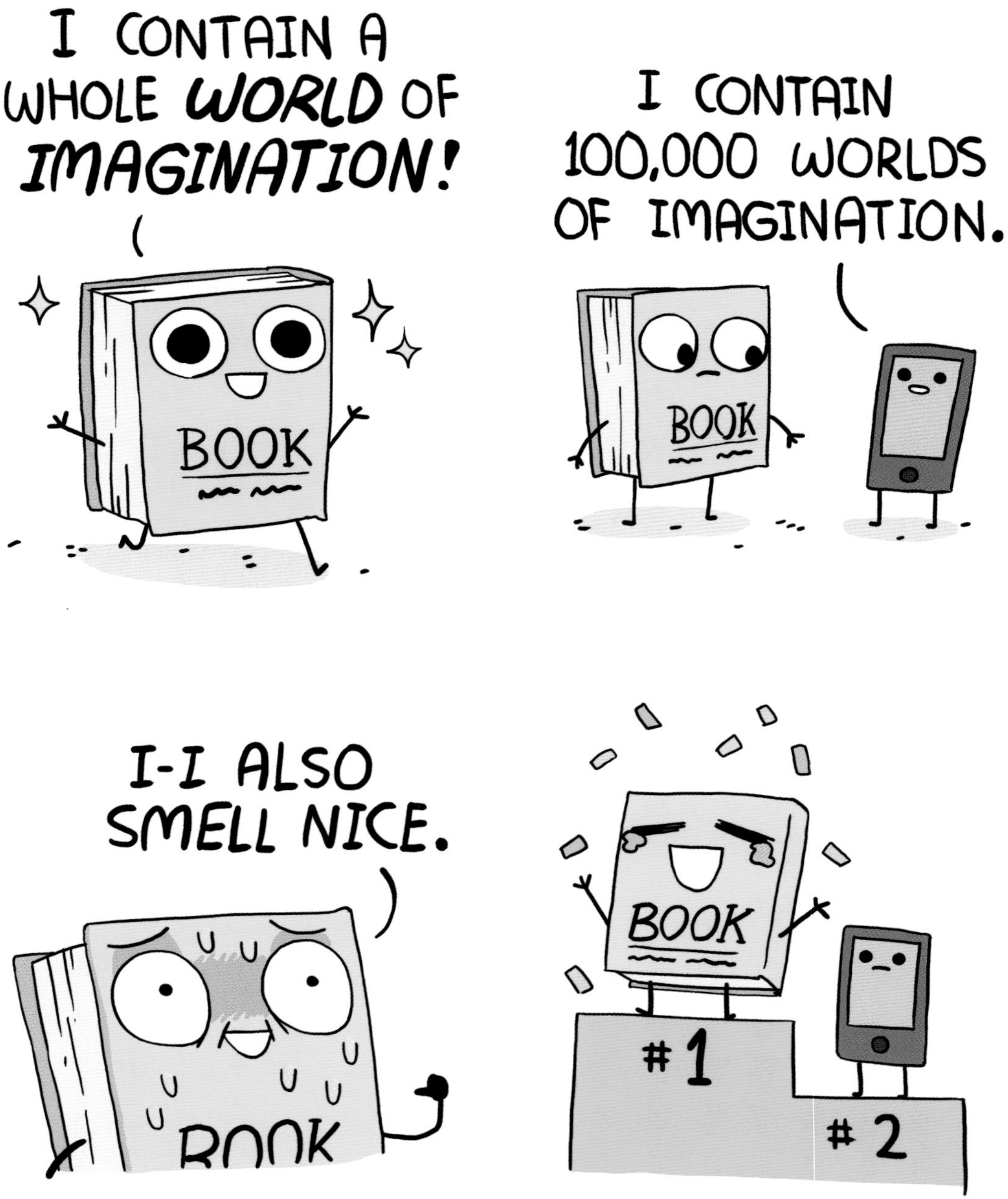
I CONTAIN A WHOLE WORLD OF IMAGINATION!
BOOK
I CONTAIN 100,000 WORLDS OF IMAGINATION.
BOOK
I-I ALSO SMELL NICE.
BOOK
#1
#2

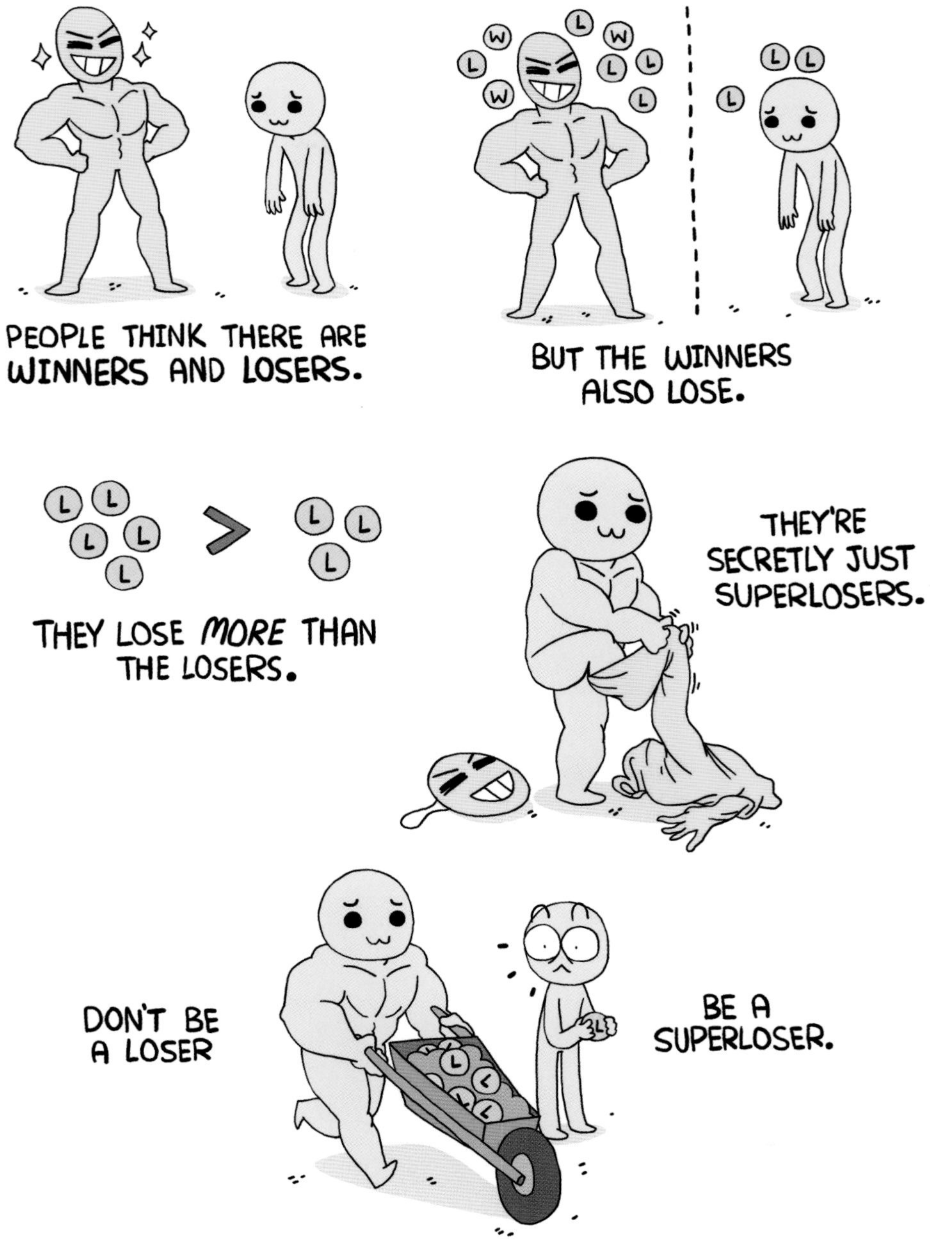
PEOPLE THINK THERE ARE WINNERS AND LOSERS.
BUT THE WINNERS ALSO LOSE.
THEY LOSE MORE THAN THE LOSERS.
THEY'RE SECRETLY JUST SUPERLOSERS.
DON'T BE A LOSER
BE A SUPERLOSER.

KNOCK
KNOCK
KNOCK
DEATH

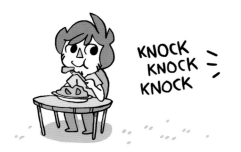

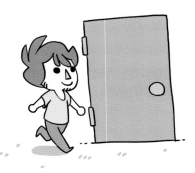

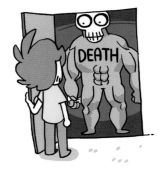

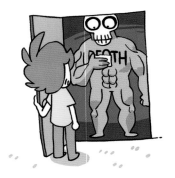

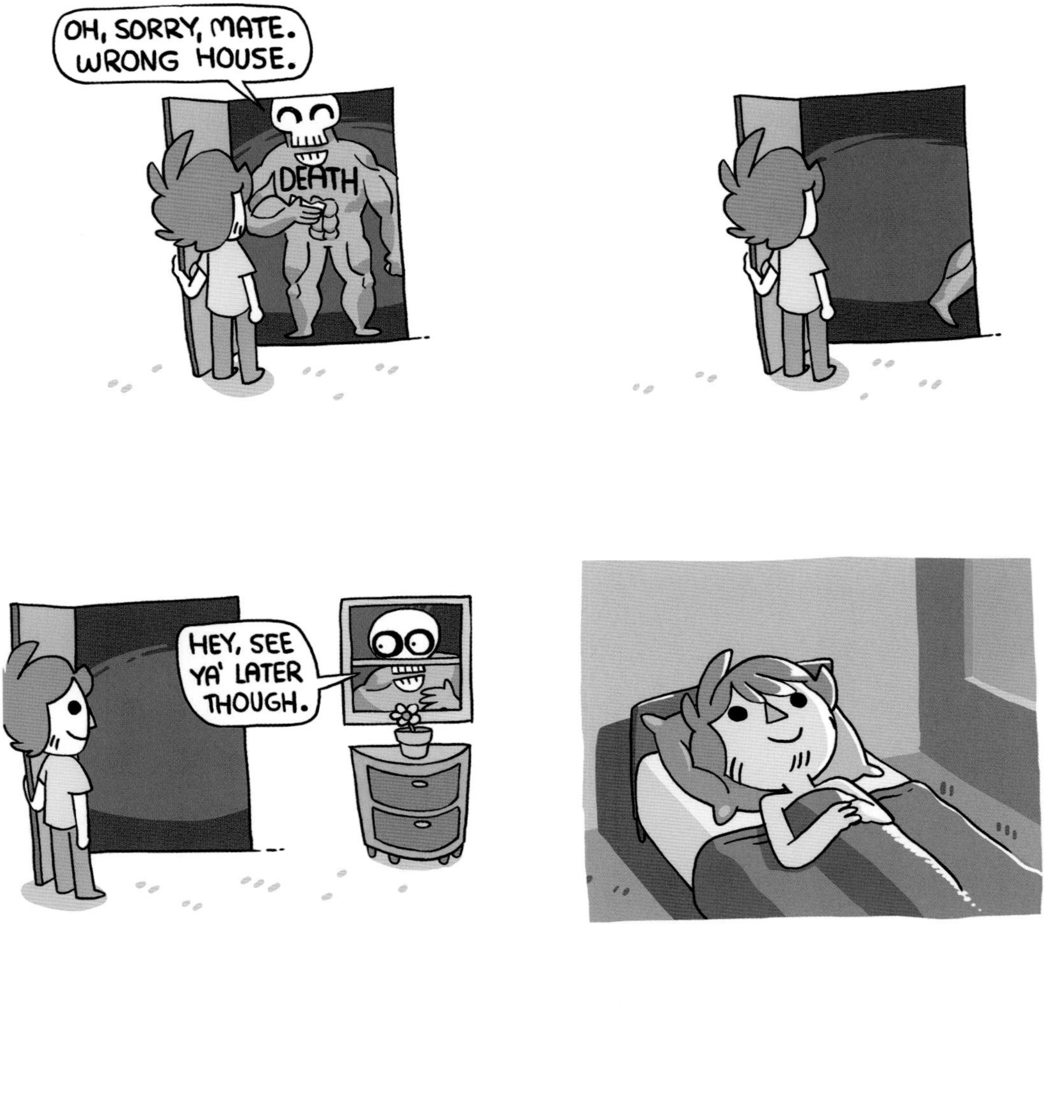
OH, SORRY, MATE. WRONG HOUSE.
DEATH
HEY, SEE YA' LATER THOUGH.

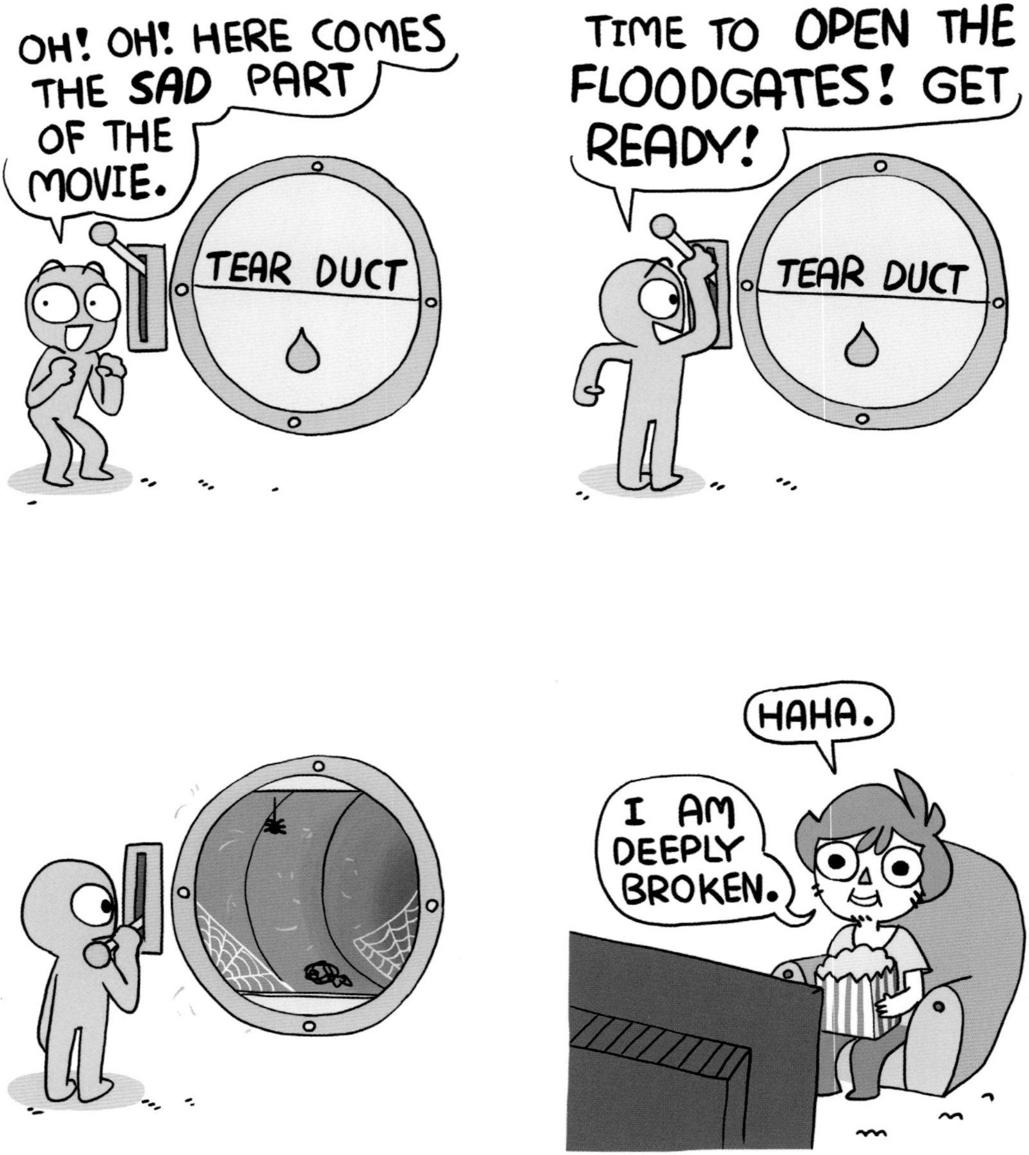
OH! OH! HERE COMES THE SAD PART OF THE MOVIE.
TEAR DUCT
TIME TO OPEN THE FLOODGATES! GET READY!
TEAR DUCT
HAHA.
I AM DEEPLY BROKEN.

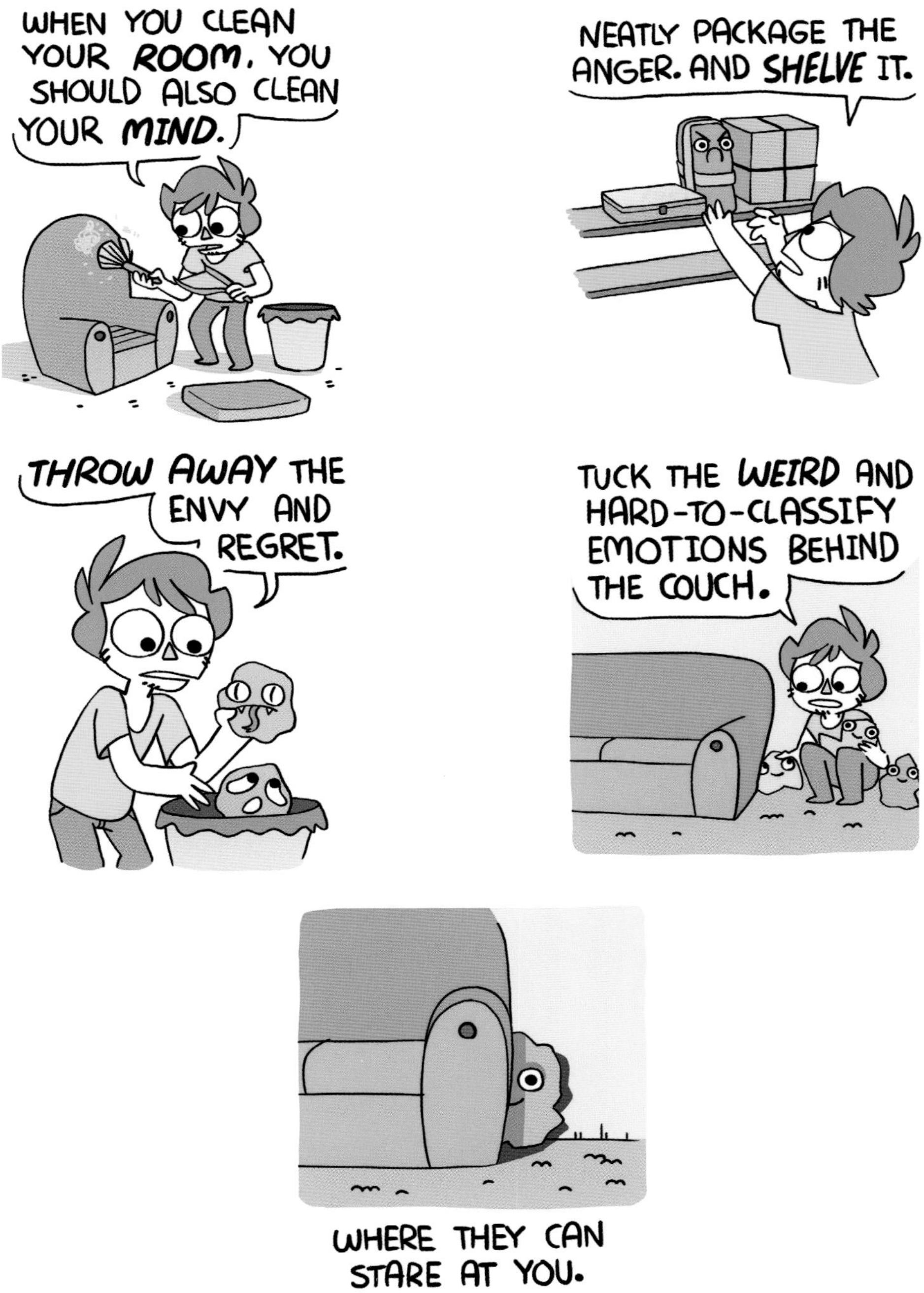
WHEN YOU CLEAN YOUR ROOM, YOU SHOULD ALSO CLEAN YOUR MIND.
NEATLY PACKAGE THE ANGER. AND SHELVE IT.
THROW AWAY THE ENVY AND REGRET.
TUCK THE WEIRD AND HARD-TO-CLASSIFY EMOTIONS BEHIND THE COUCH.
WHERE THEY CAN STARE AT YOU.

BATH BOMBS ARE PRETTY COOL, BUT THEY'RE ONLY MARKETED TOWARD WOMEN.

I HAVE AN IDEA FOR A BATH BOMB MARKETED TO MEN.

THE MAN-BOMB

FIRST, THE WATER LIGHTS ON FIRE.

THEN IT TURNS
COMPLETELY BLACK.

THEN DEMONS COME
OUT OF IT.

THESE REPRESENT YOUR
INNER DEMONS, AND YOU
MUST FIGHT THEM.

THEN IT TURNS ALL
PINK & GIRLY.

BECAUSE DEFYING GENDER
EXPECTATIONS IS THE
MANLIEST THING OF ALL.

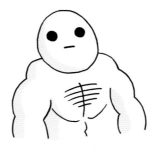

THIS IS YOUR FINAL
INNER DEMON.

GOOD LUCK.

WRESTLERS ALL HAVE THESE BIG, BAD, "TOUGH GUY" ENTRANCES.

BUT IT'S ALL A FRONT. IT'S ALL JUST GRANDIOSE POSTURING.

IF *I* WERE A WRESTLER, I WOULDN'T TRY TO INTIMIDATE AT ALL.

JUST TO SHOW THAT I DON'T *HAVE* TO.

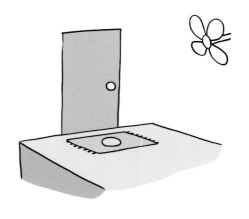

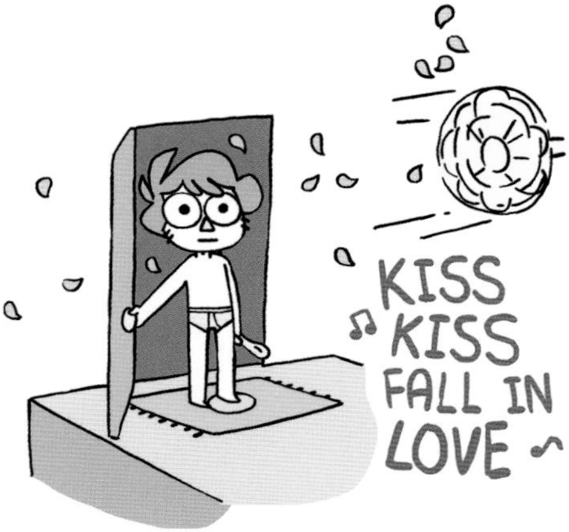
KISS KISS FALL IN LOVE

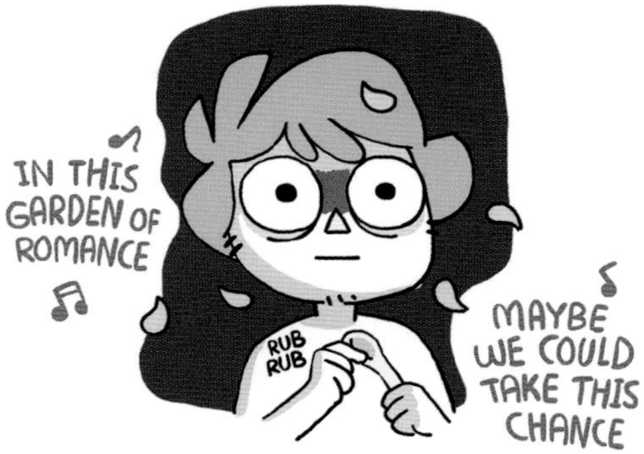
IN THIS GARDEN OF ROMANCE
RUB RUB
MAYBE WE COULD TAKE THIS CHANCE

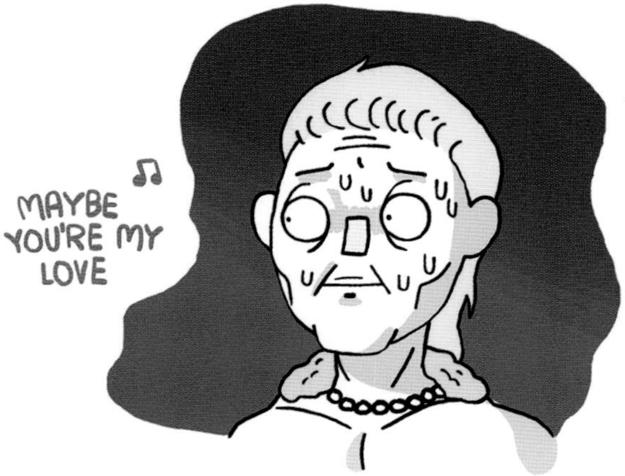
MAYBE YOU'RE MY LOVE

THEY WOULD KNOW DEATH APPROACHES.

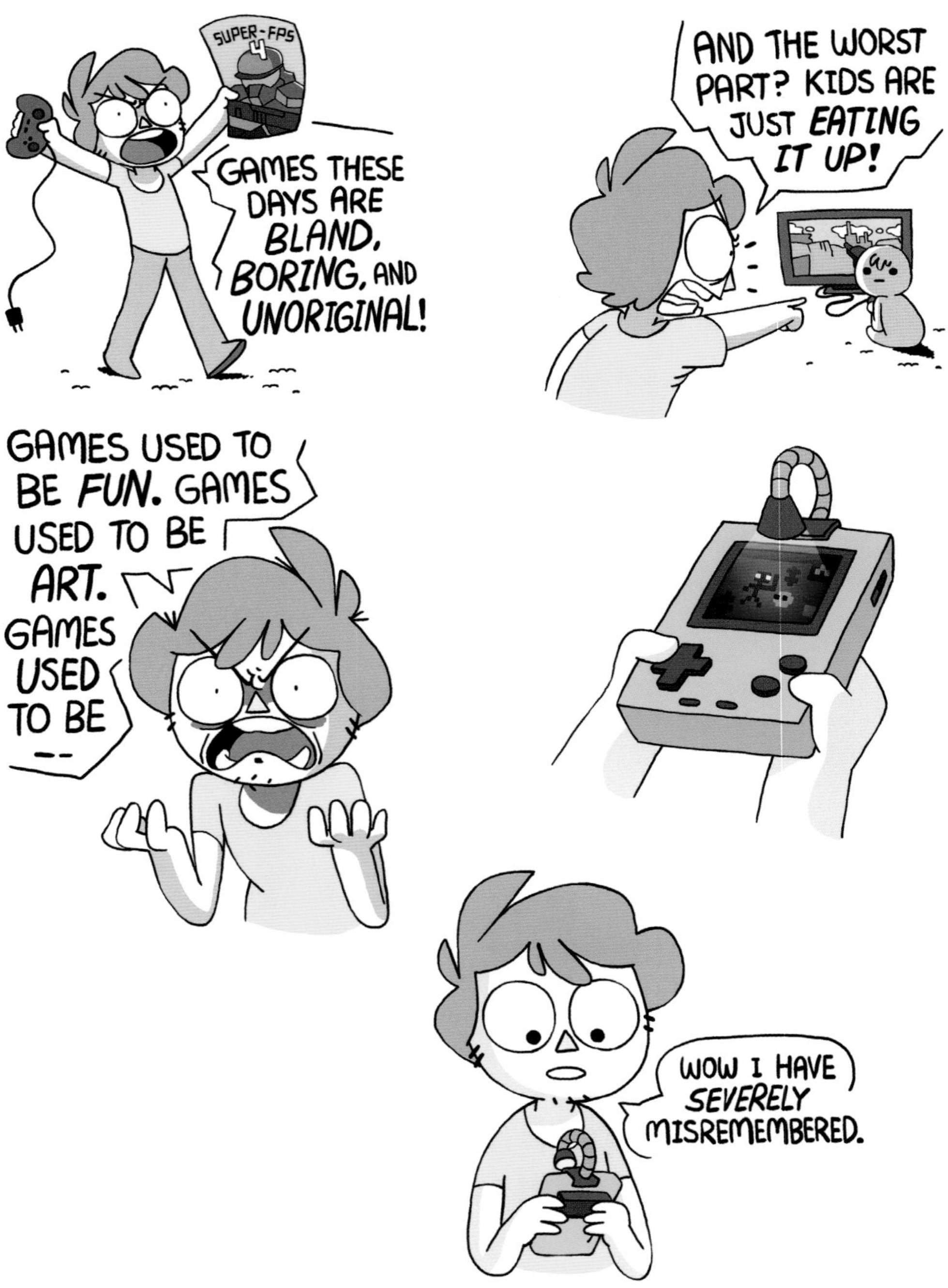
SUPER-FPS 4
GAMES THESE DAYS ARE BLAND, BORING, AND UNORIGINAL!
AND THE WORST PART? KIDS ARE JUST EATING IT UP!
GAMES USED TO BE FUN. GAMES USED TO BE ART.
GAMES USED TO BE --
WOW I HAVE SEVERELY MISREMEMBERED.

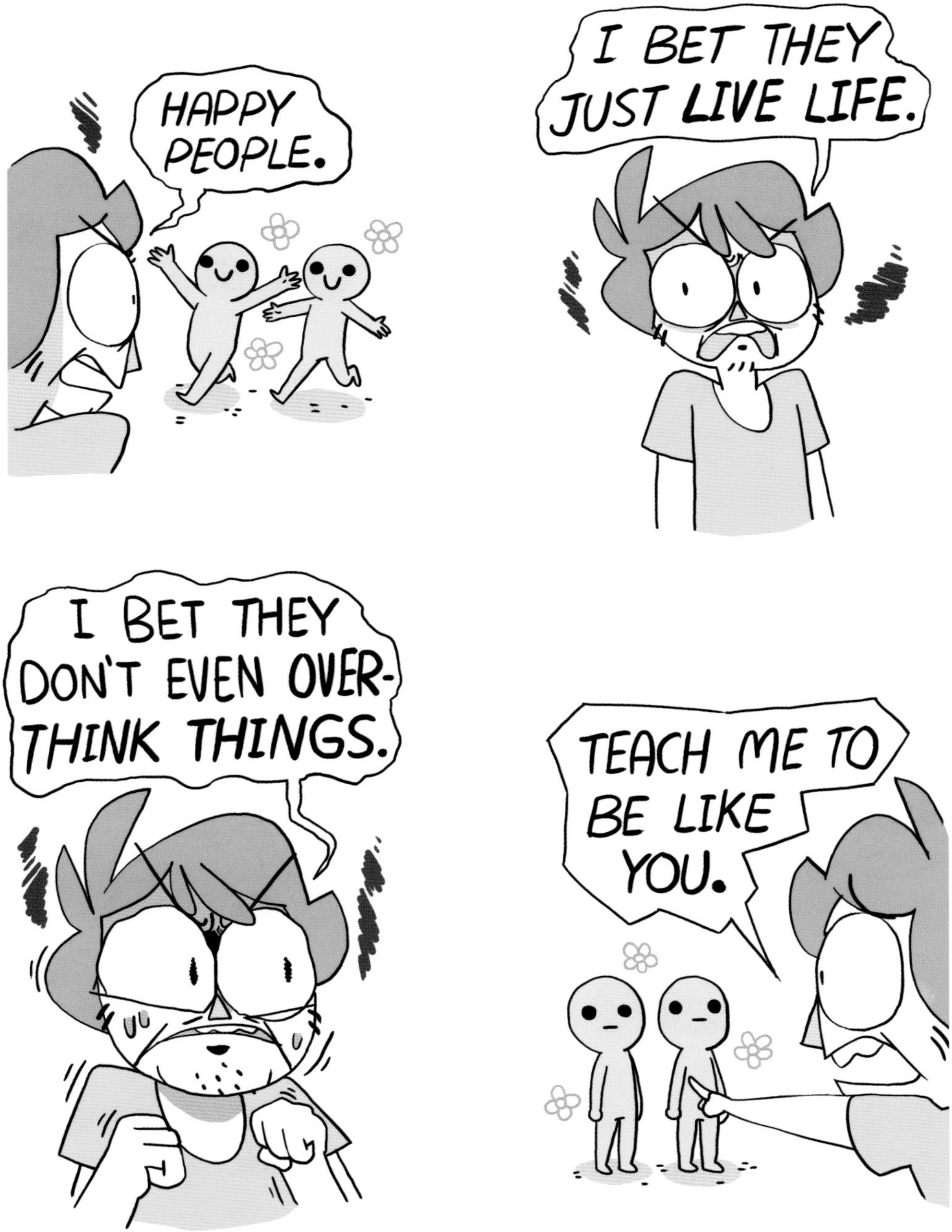
HAPPY PEOPLE.
I BET THEY JUST LIVE LIFE.
I BET THEY DON'T EVEN OVER-THINK THINGS.
TEACH ME TO BE LIKE YOU.

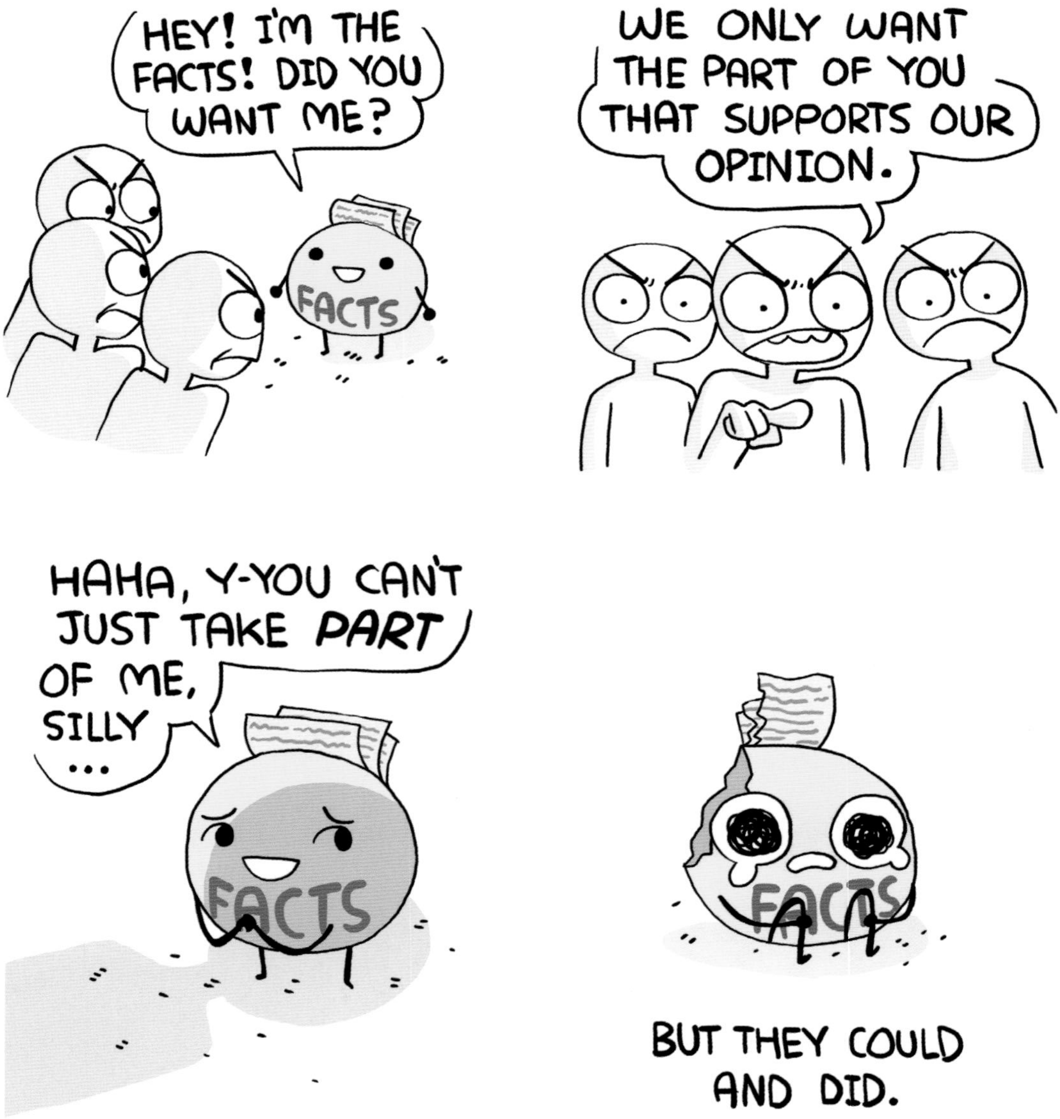
HEY! I'M THE FACTS! DID YOU WANT ME?
FACTS
WE ONLY WANT THE PART OF YOU THAT SUPPORTS OUR OPINION.
HAHA, Y-YOU CAN'T JUST TAKE *PART* OF ME, SILLY ...
FACTS
FACTS
BUT THEY COULD AND DID.

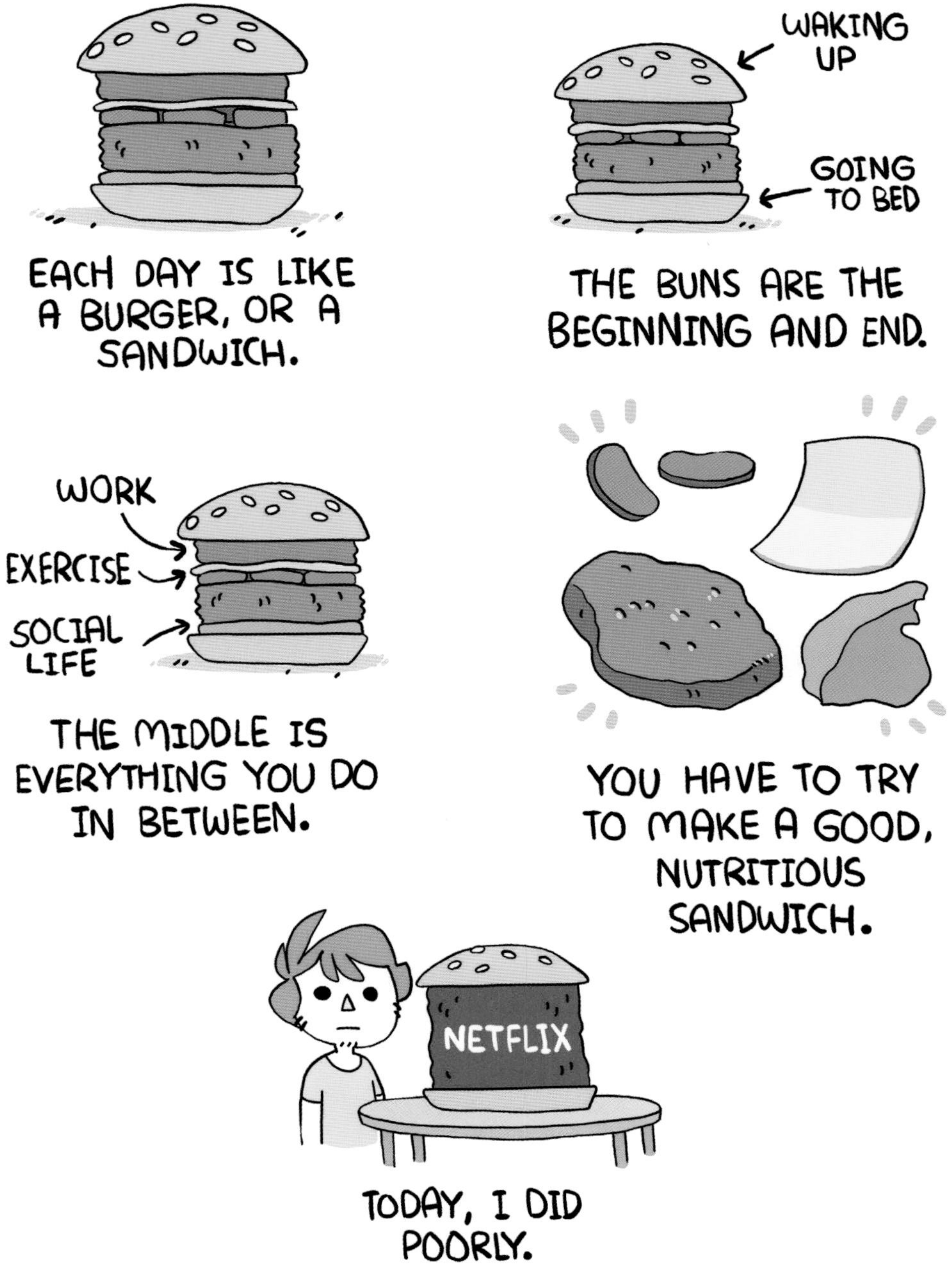
EACH DAY IS LIKE A BURGER, OR A SANDWICH.
WAKING UP
GOING TO BED
THE BUNS ARE THE BEGINNING AND END.
WORK
EXERCISE
SOCIAL LIFE
THE MIDDLE IS EVERYTHING YOU DO IN BETWEEN.
YOU HAVE TO TRY TO MAKE A GOOD, NUTRITIOUS SANDWICH.
NETFLIX
TODAY, I DID POORLY.

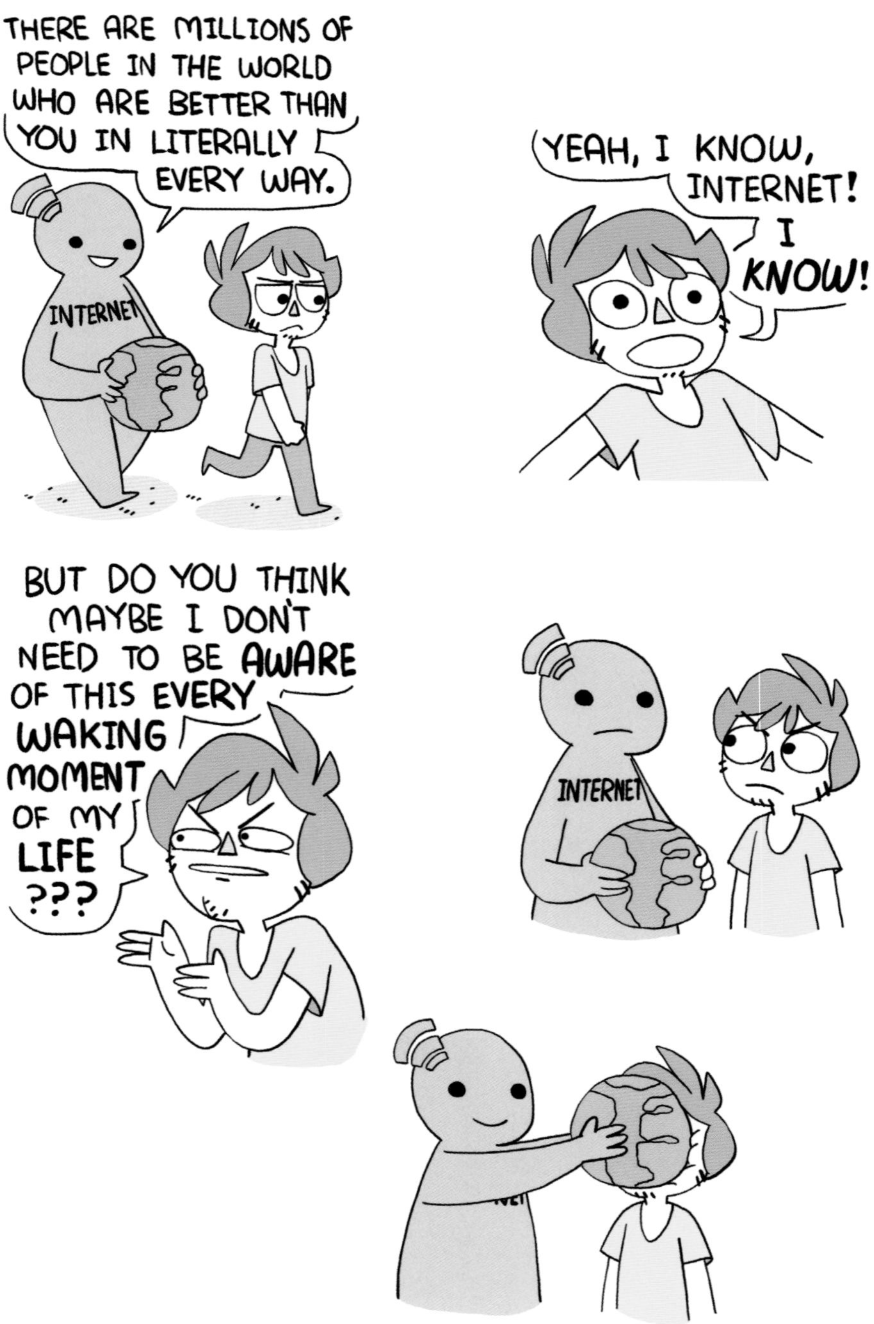
THERE ARE MILLIONS OF PEOPLE IN THE WORLD WHO ARE BETTER THAN YOU IN LITERALLY EVERY WAY.
INTERNET
YEAH, I KNOW, INTERNET! I KNOW!
BUT DO YOU THINK MAYBE I DON'T NEED TO BE AWARE OF THIS EVERY WAKING MOMENT OF MY LIFE ???
INTERNET

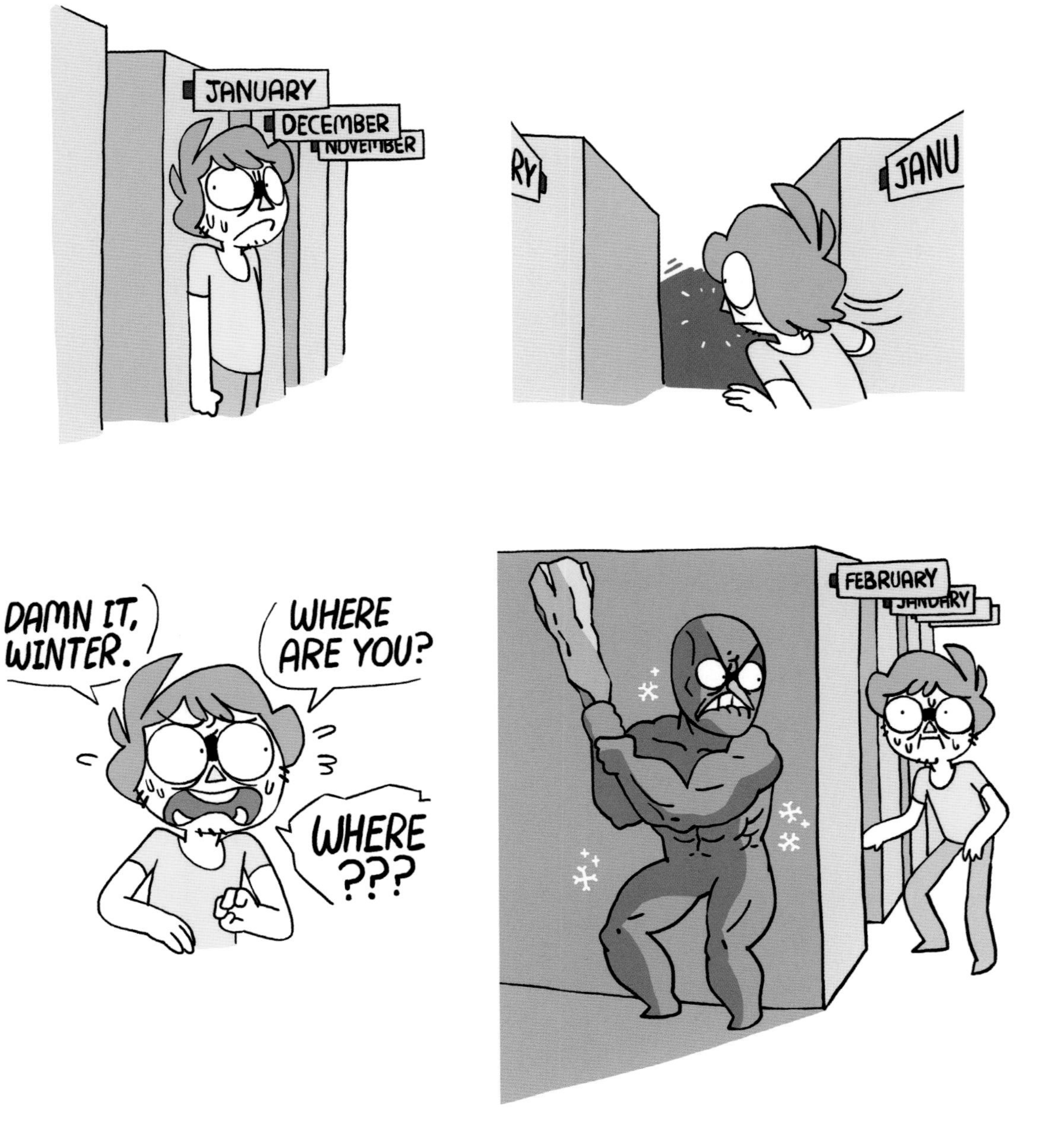
JANUARY
DECEMBER
NOVEMBER
RY
JANU
DAMN IT, WINTER.
WHERE ARE YOU?
WHERE ???
FEBRUARY
JANUARY

I'M SCARED THAT WE'RE ALL GONNA BE **CYBORGS** SOON.

MEMORY EXTENSION

ROBOTIC EYE

NAVIGATION SYSTEM

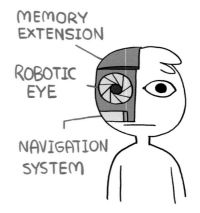

WE'LL HAVE TECHNOLOGY FUSED TO OUR BODY AND MIND.

HAHA, DON'T WORRY! PEOPLE WILL **NEVER** BE **THAT** ATTACHED TO TECHNOLOGY.

MEMORY EXTENSION

ROBOTIC EYE

NAVIGATION SYSTEM

ALRIGHT, DUDE. WE ALL HAVE FLAWS.
SO LET'S JUST BE TOTALLY OPEN WITH EACH OTHER.
OKAY.
ZIIIIP
ZIII--
ZIIIP

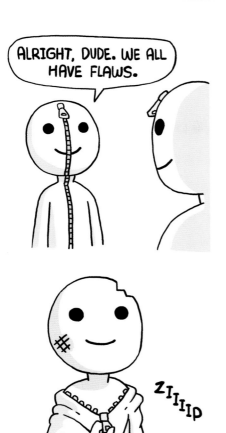

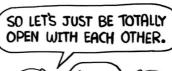

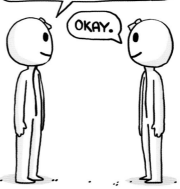

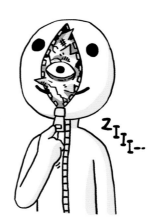

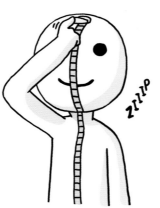

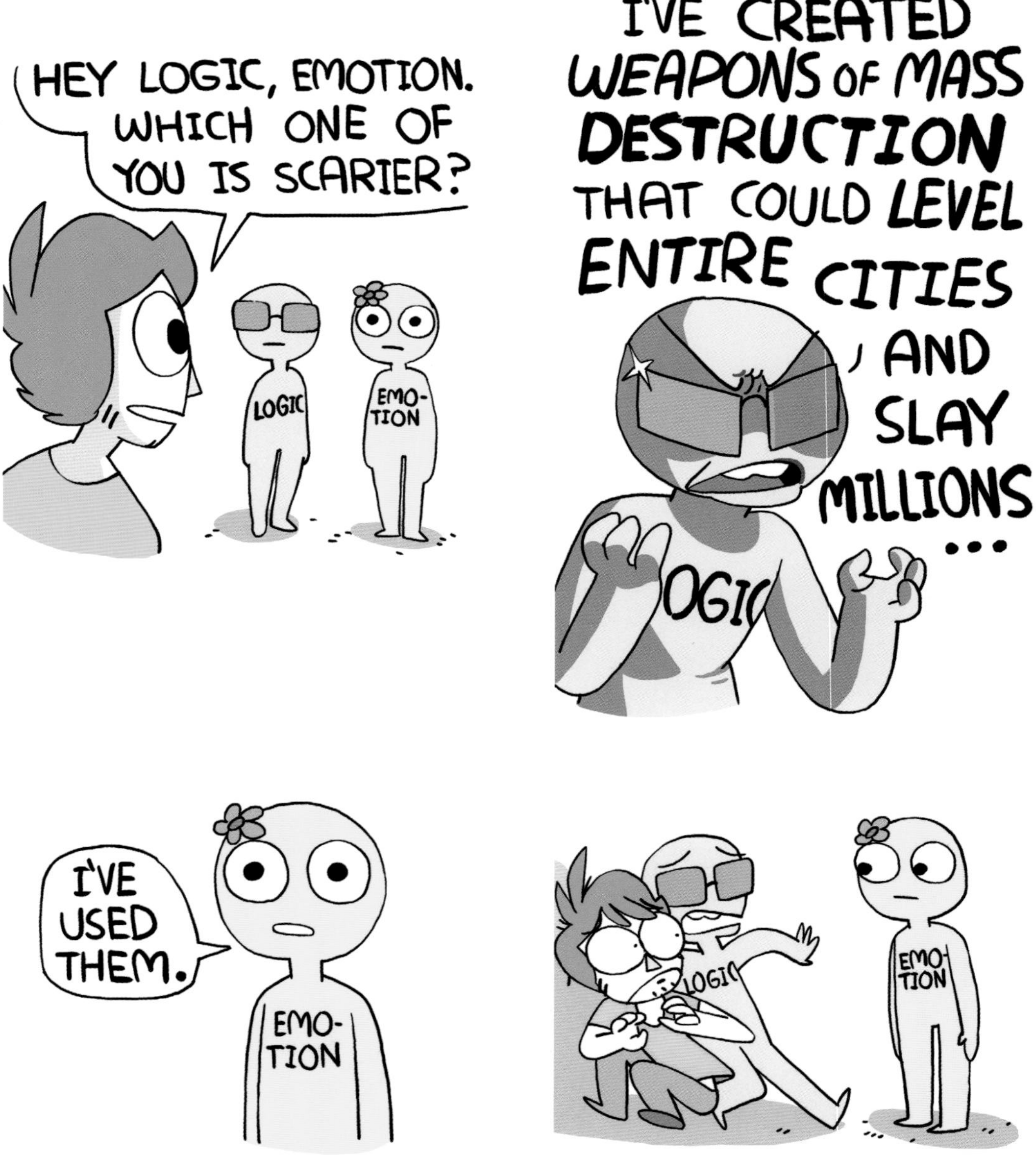
HEY LOGIC, EMOTION. WHICH ONE OF YOU IS SCARIER?
LOGIC
EMO-
TION
I'VE CREATED WEAPONS OF MASS DESTRUCTION THAT COULD LEVEL ENTIRE CITIES, AND SLAY MILLIONS ...
I'VE USED THEM.
EMO-
TION
EMO-
TION

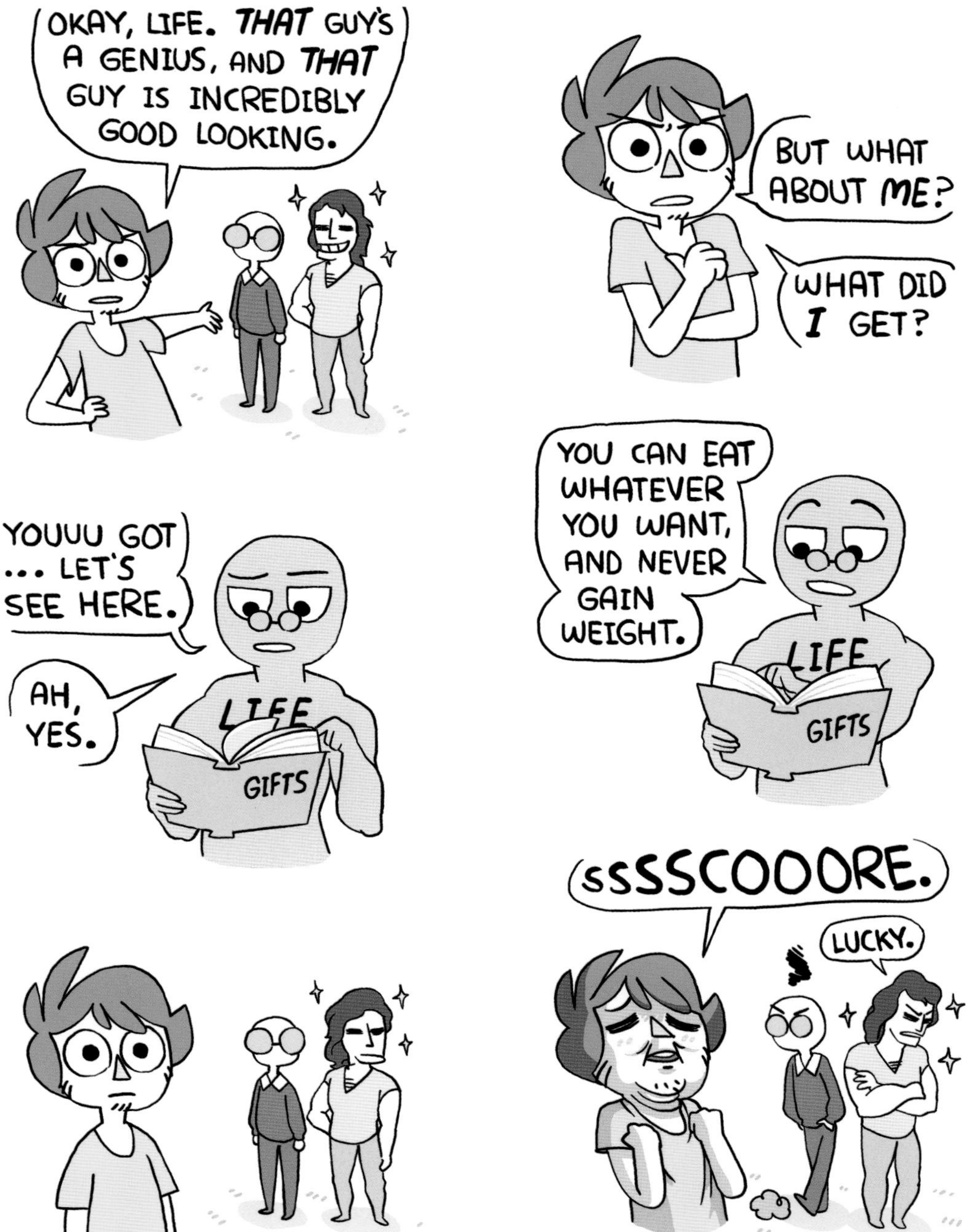
OKAY, LIFE. THAT GUY'S A GENIUS, AND THAT GUY IS INCREDIBLY GOOD LOOKING.
BUT WHAT ABOUT ME?
WHAT DID I GET?
YOUUU GOT ... LET'S SEE HERE.
AH, YES.
LIFE
GIFTS
YOU CAN EAT WHATEVER YOU WANT, AND NEVER GAIN WEIGHT.
LIFE
GIFTS
sSSSCOOORE.
LUCKY.

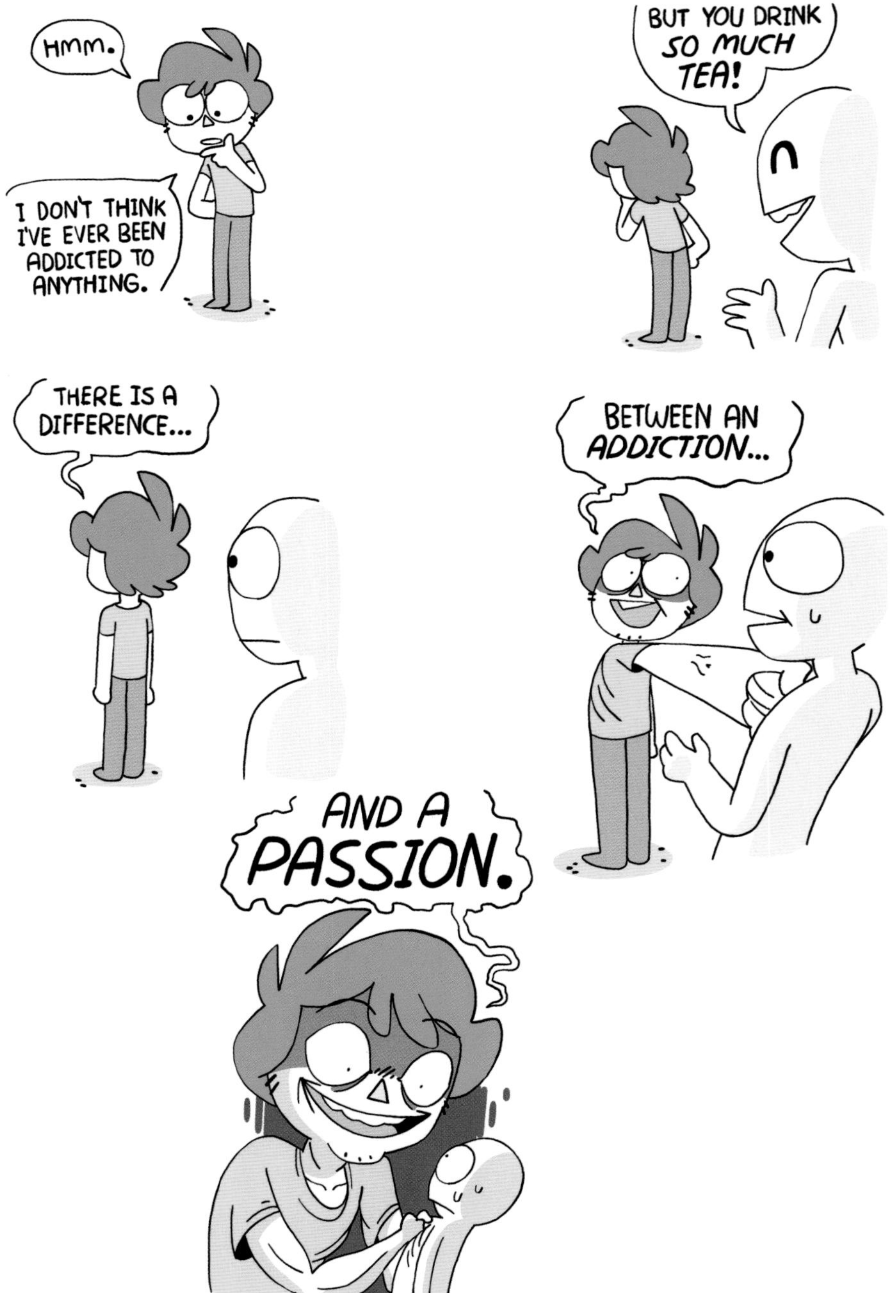
HMM.
I DON'T THINK I'VE EVER BEEN ADDICTED TO ANYTHING.
BUT YOU DRINK SO MUCH TEA!
THERE IS A DIFFERENCE...
BETWEEN AN ADDICTION...
AND A PASSION.

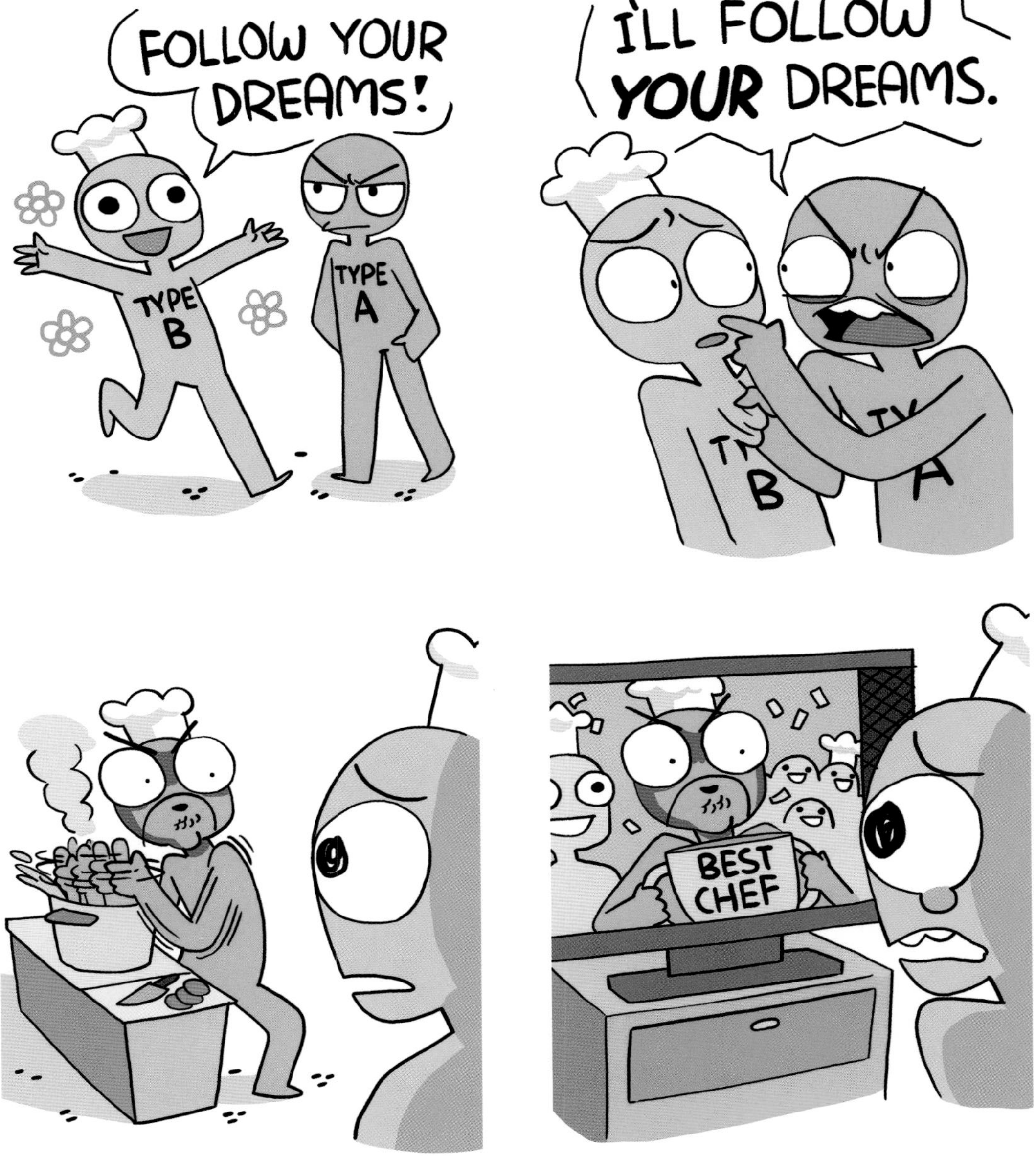
FOLLOW YOUR DREAMS!
TYPE B
TYPE A
I'LL FOLLOW YOUR DREAMS.
B
A
BEST CHEF

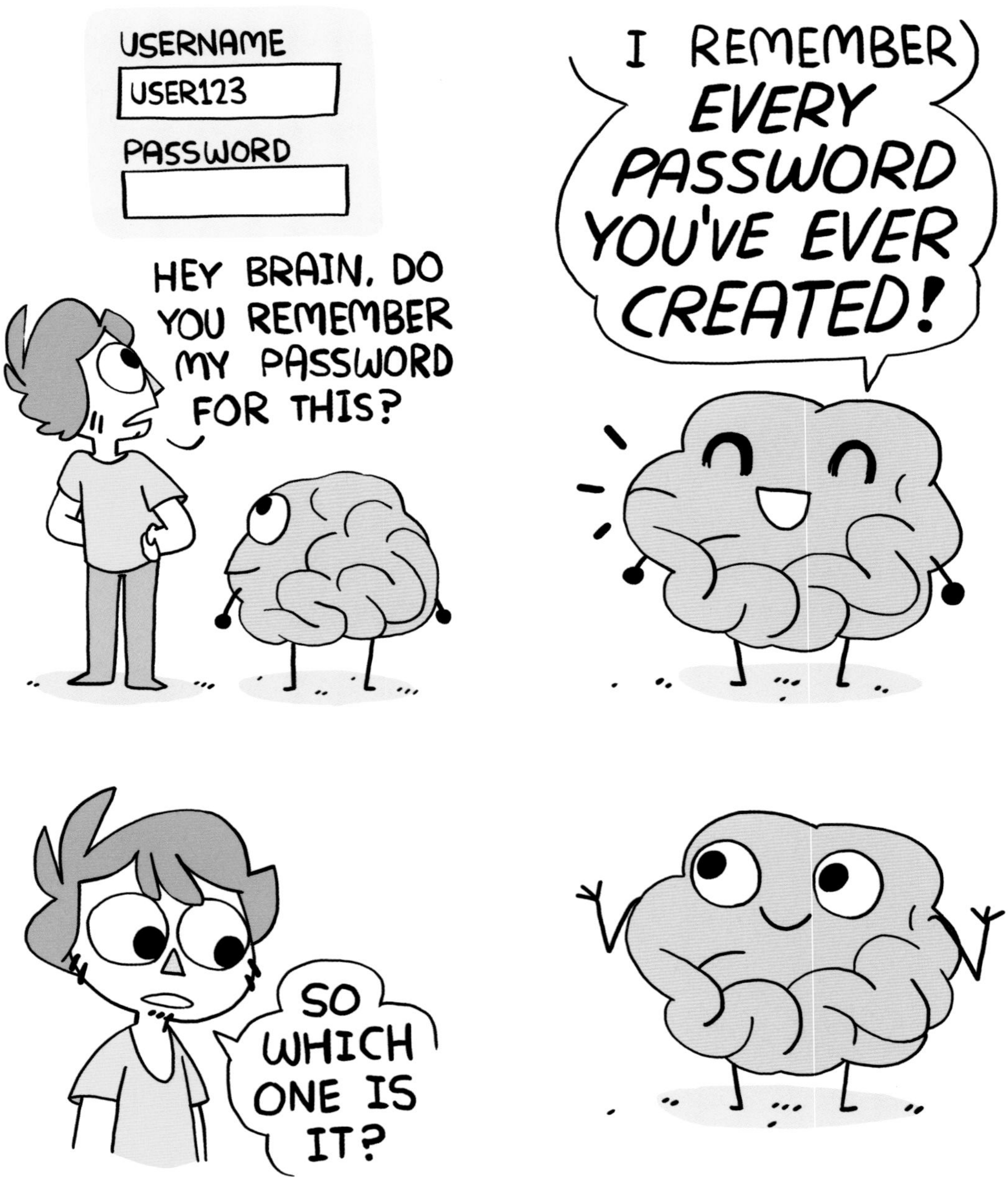
USERNAME
USER123
PASSWORD
HEY BRAIN, DO YOU REMEMBER MY PASSWORD FOR THIS?
I REMEMBER EVERY PASSWORD YOU'VE EVER CREATED!
SO WHICH ONE IS IT?

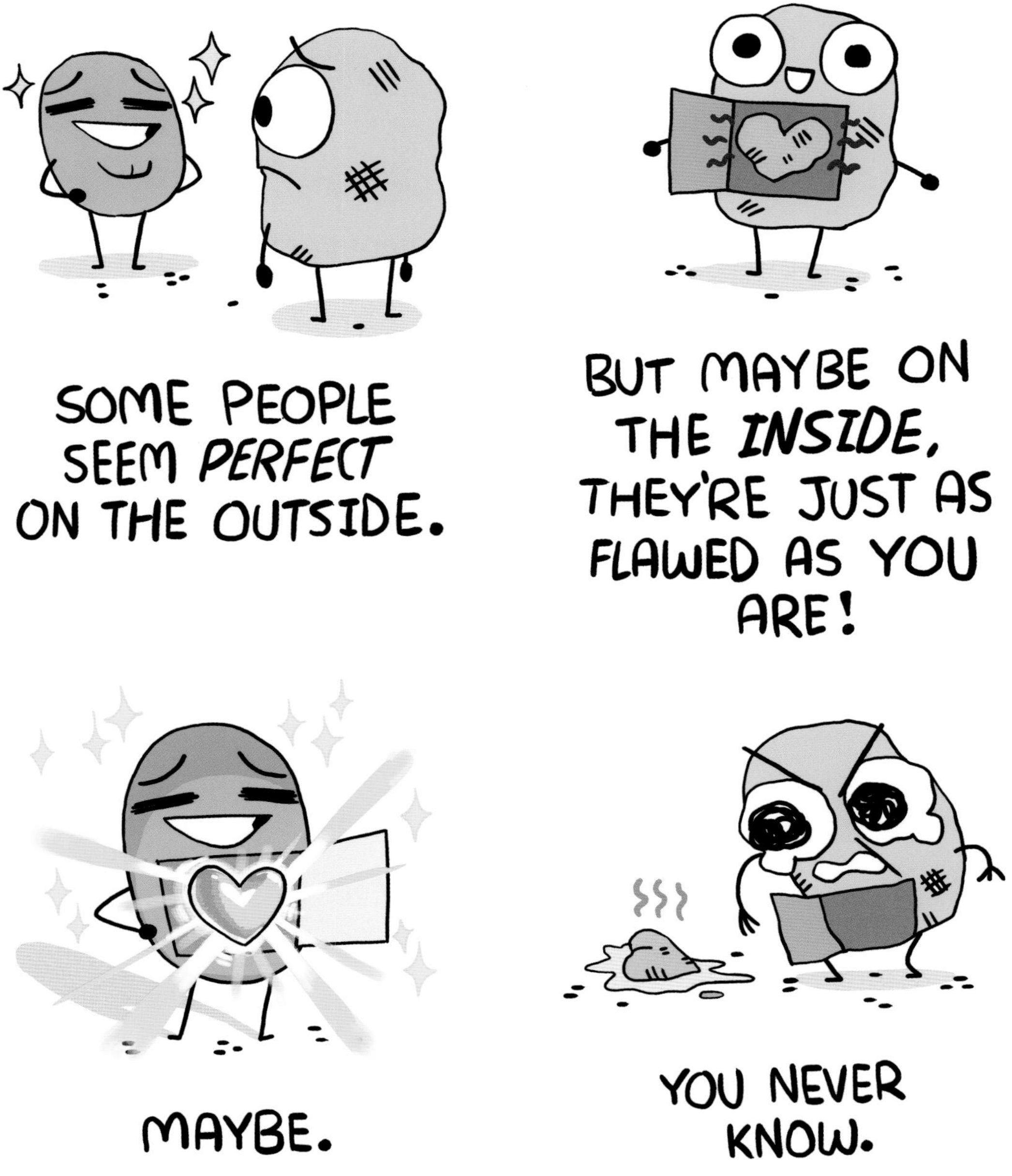
SOME PEOPLE SEEM *PERFECT* ON THE OUTSIDE.
BUT MAYBE ON THE *INSIDE*, THEY'RE JUST AS FLAWED AS YOU ARE!
MAYBE.
YOU NEVER KNOW.

A GUIDE TO DRESS CODES

(IN ORDER OF FORMALITY)

CASUAL

SMART CASUAL

BUSINESS CASUAL

BUSINESS FORMAL

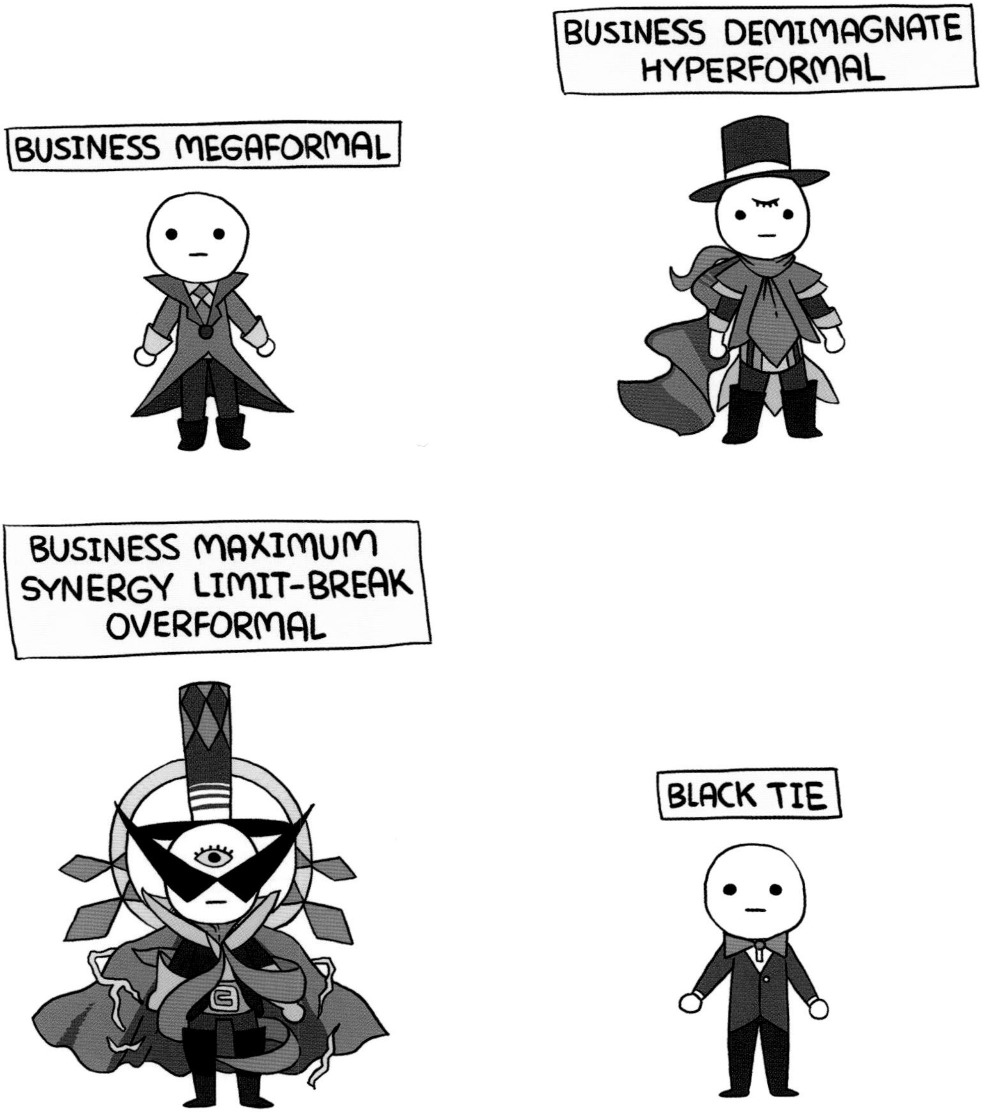
BUSINESS DEMIMAGNATE HYPERFORMAL
BUSINESS MEGAFORMAL
BUSINESS MAXIMUM SYNERGY LIMIT-BREAK OVERFORMAL
BLACK TIE

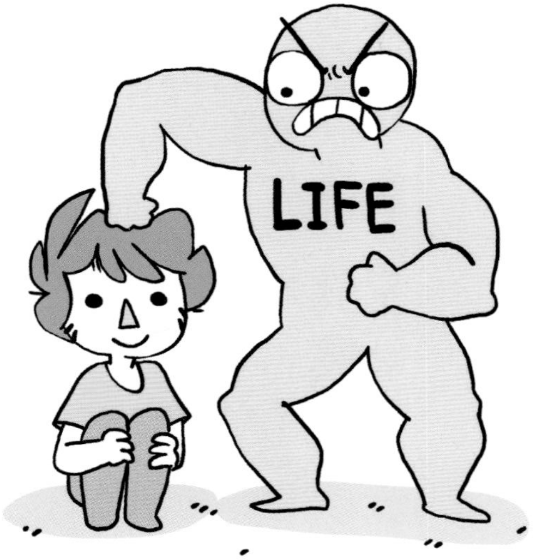
LIFE

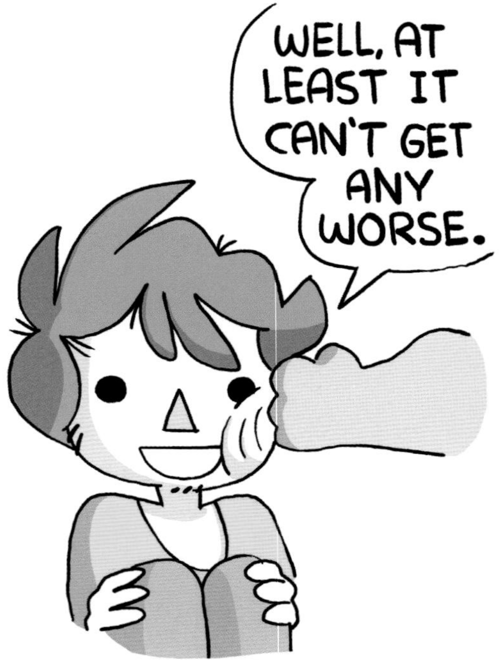
WELL, AT LEAST IT CAN'T GET ANY WORSE.

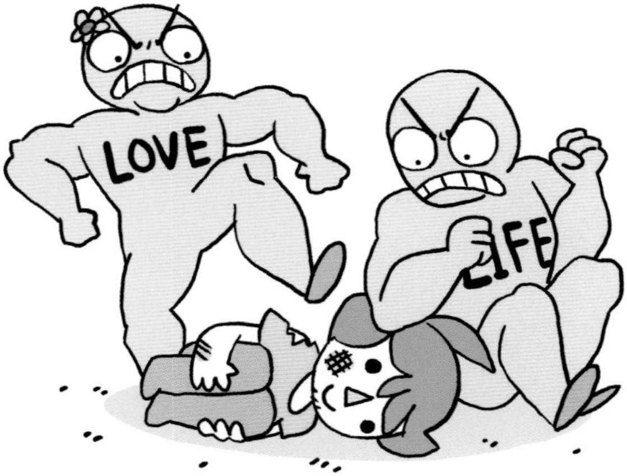
LOVE
LIFE

ME AT 15
I'M GONNA BE A COOL ADULT.
I'M GONNA BE DOWN WITH THE YOUTH.
ME AT 25

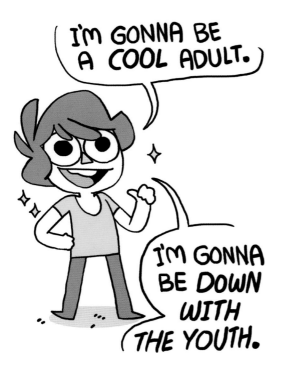

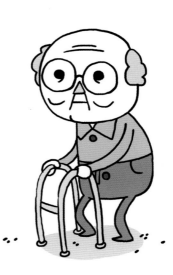

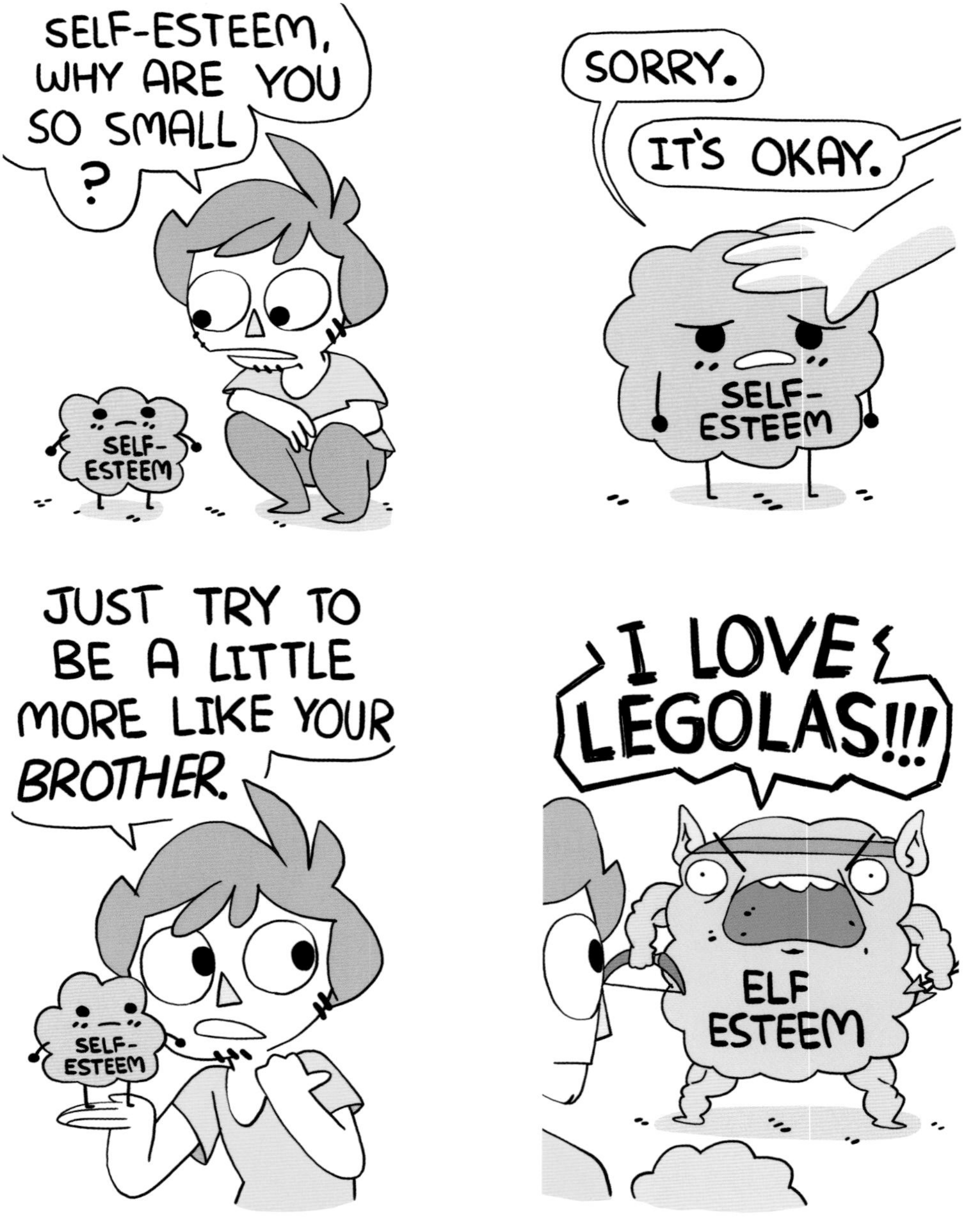
SELF-ESTEEM, WHY ARE YOU SO SMALL ?
SELF-ESTEEM
SORRY.
IT'S OKAY.
SELF-ESTEEM
JUST TRY TO BE A LITTLE MORE LIKE YOUR BROTHER.
SELF-ESTEEM
I LOVE LEGOLAS!!!
ELF ESTEEM

I LOVE FRUITS AND VEGGIES, BUT THEY ARE WAY TOO RESTLESS.

ONE DAY THEY'LL BE YELLING:

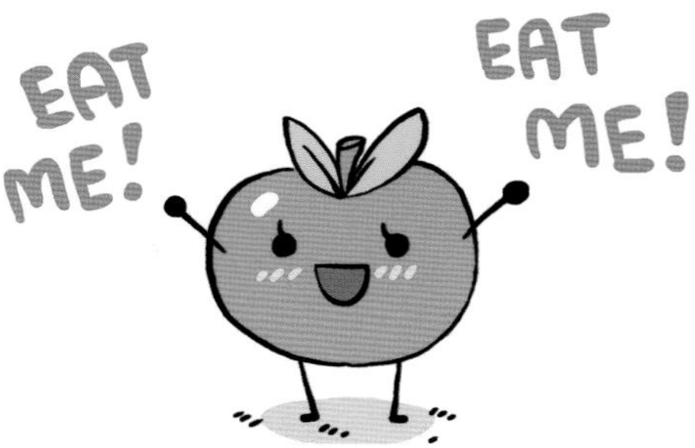
EAT ME!
EAT ME!

AND THEN THE NEXT DAY, THEY'LL JUST LEAVE.

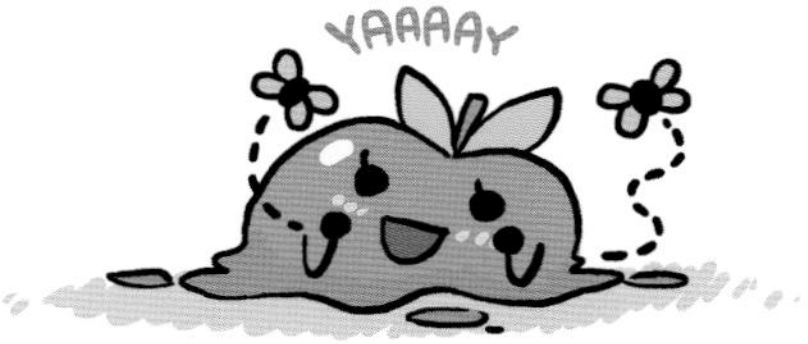
YAAAAY

AS LONG AS SOMEBODY EATS THEM, THEY DON'T CARE WHO.

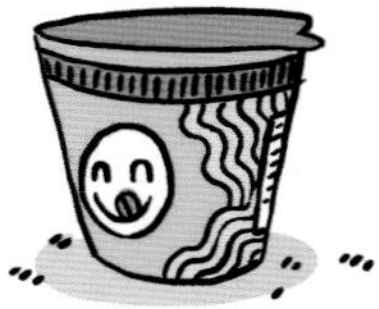

BUT WOULD CUP RAMEN EVER BETRAY ME LIKE THAT?

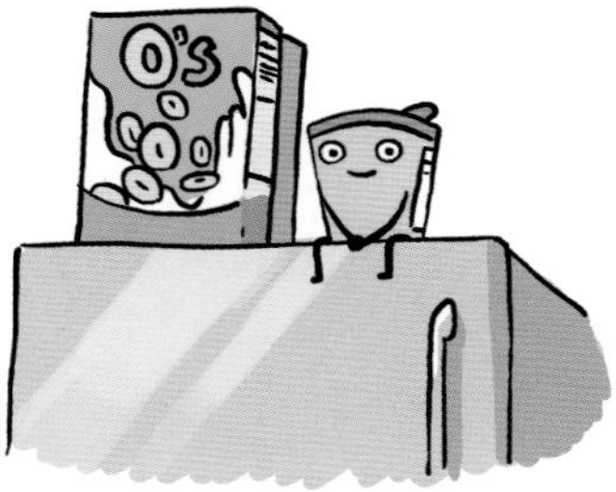
O's

NO.
CUP RAMEN WOULD WAIT.

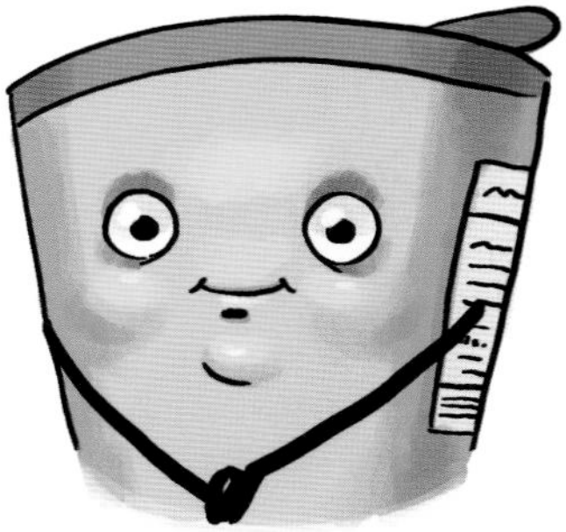

CUP RAMEN IS PATIENT.

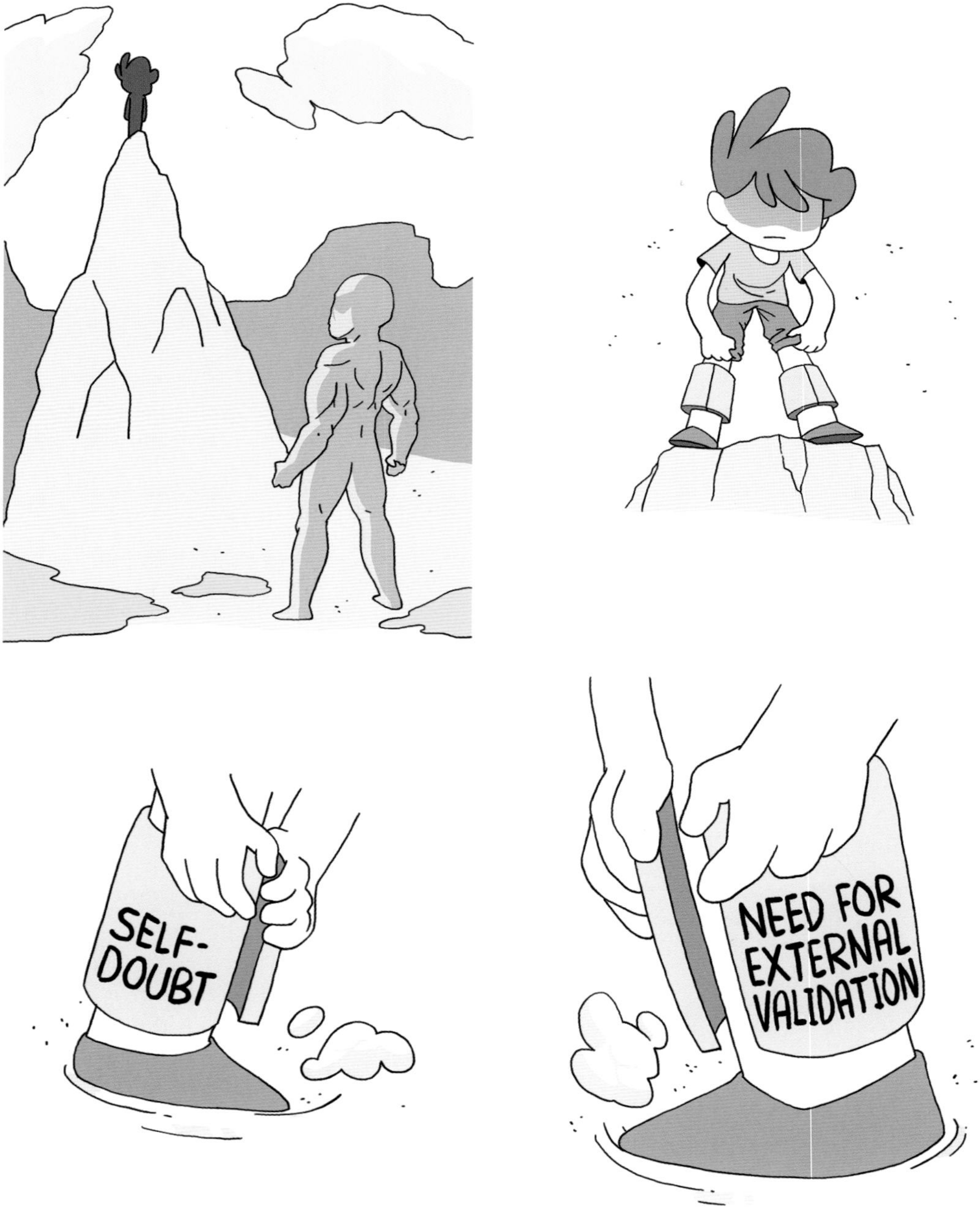
SELF-
DOUBT
NEED FOR
EXTERNAL
VALIDATION

YOU REALLY THINK YOU STAND A CHANCE AGAINST ME, JUST BECAUSE YOU TOOK OFF A FEW *SMALL WEIGHTS* ??

LIFE

BOOOOOM

HELLO, MY LOVE! WE FIT TOGETHER LIKE PUZZLE PIECES!
OH... WE ACTUALLY DON'T FIT TOGETHER.
WHATEVER.

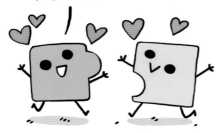

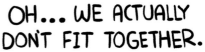

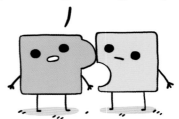

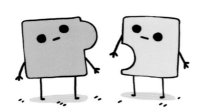

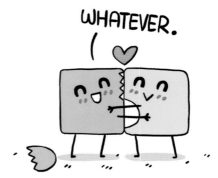

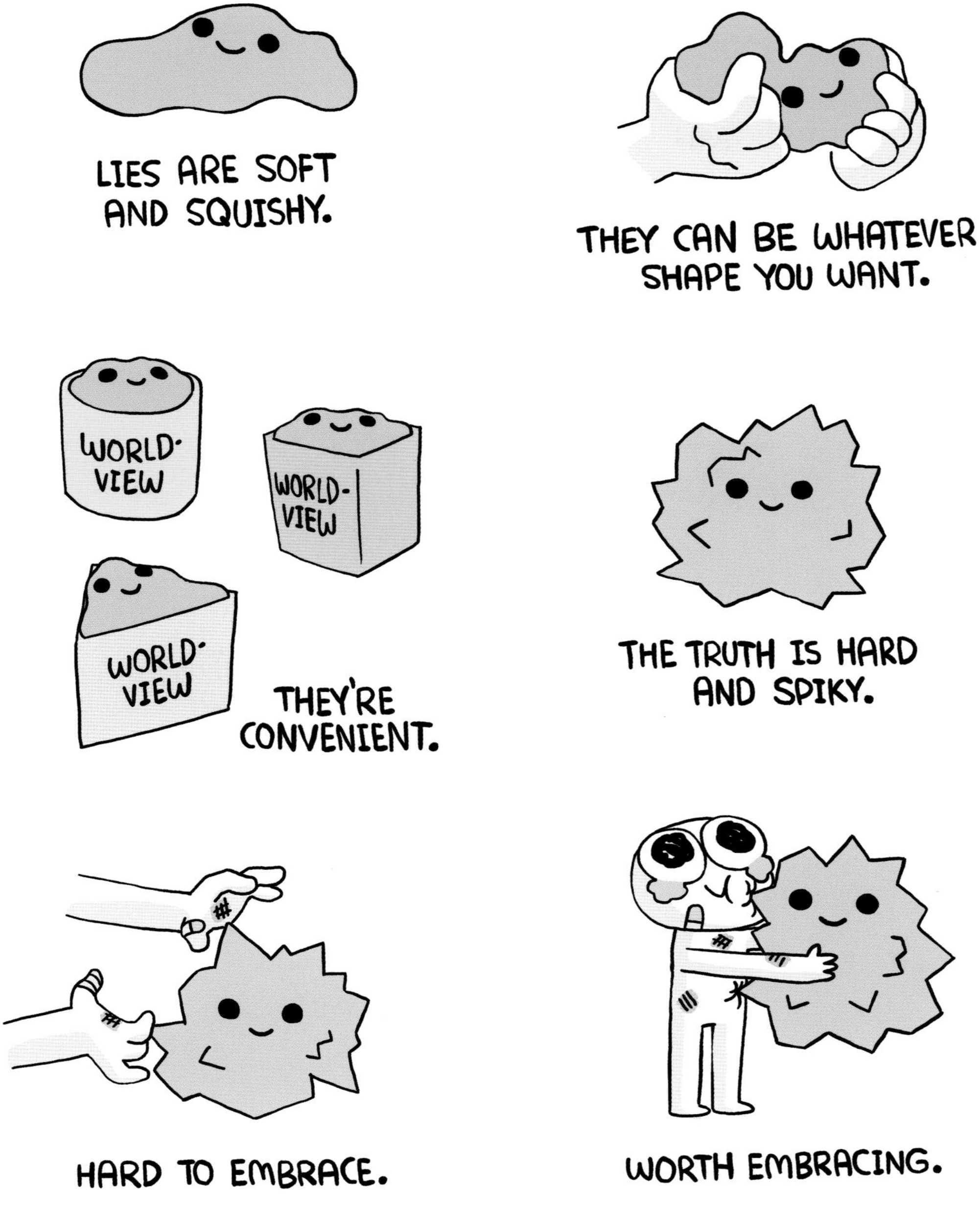
LIES ARE SOFT AND SQUISHY.
THEY CAN BE WHATEVER SHAPE YOU WANT.
WORLD-VIEW
WORLD-VIEW
WORLD-VIEW
THEY'RE CONVENIENT.
THE TRUTH IS HARD AND SPIKY.
HARD TO EMBRACE.
WORTH EMBRACING.

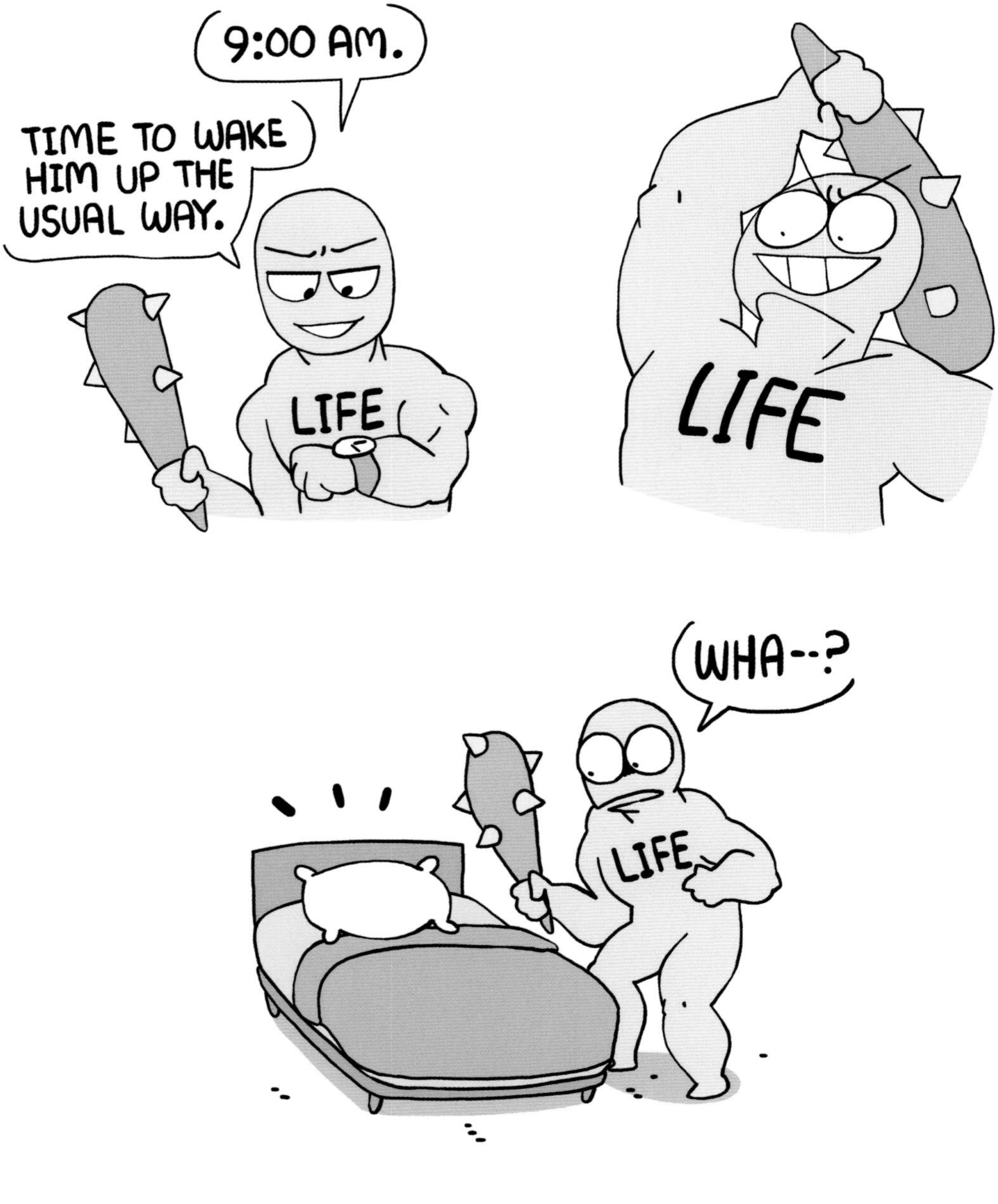
9:00 AM.
TIME TO WAKE HIM UP THE USUAL WAY.
LIFE
LIFE
WHA--?
LIFE

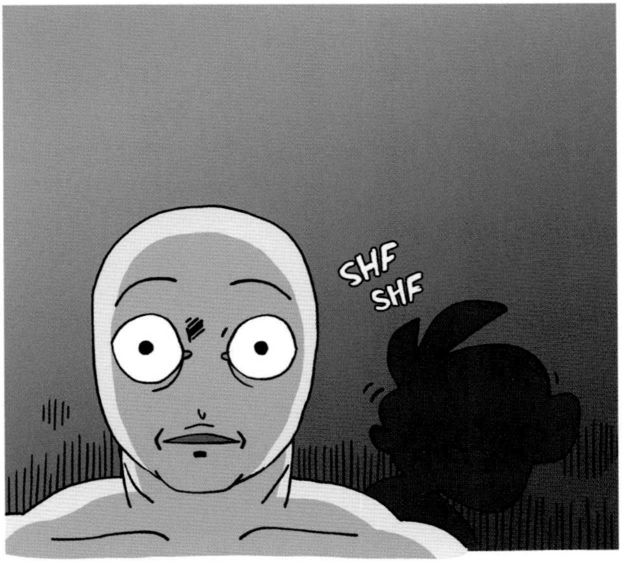
SHF
SHF

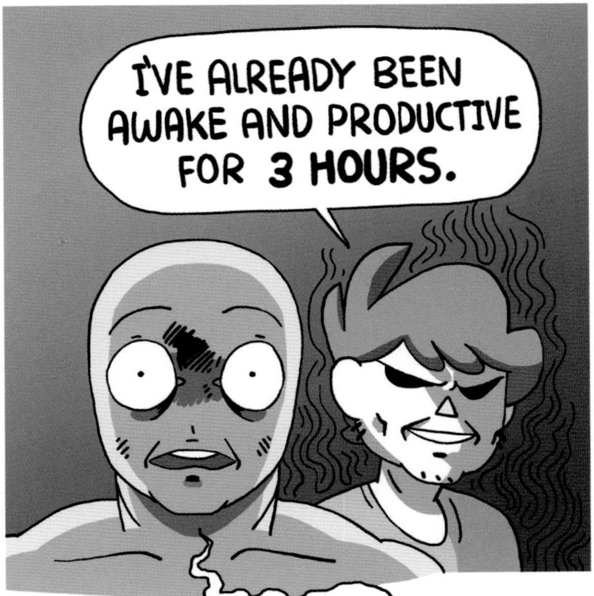
I'VE ALREADY BEEN AWAKE AND PRODUCTIVE FOR 3 HOURS.
IMPOSSIBLE...

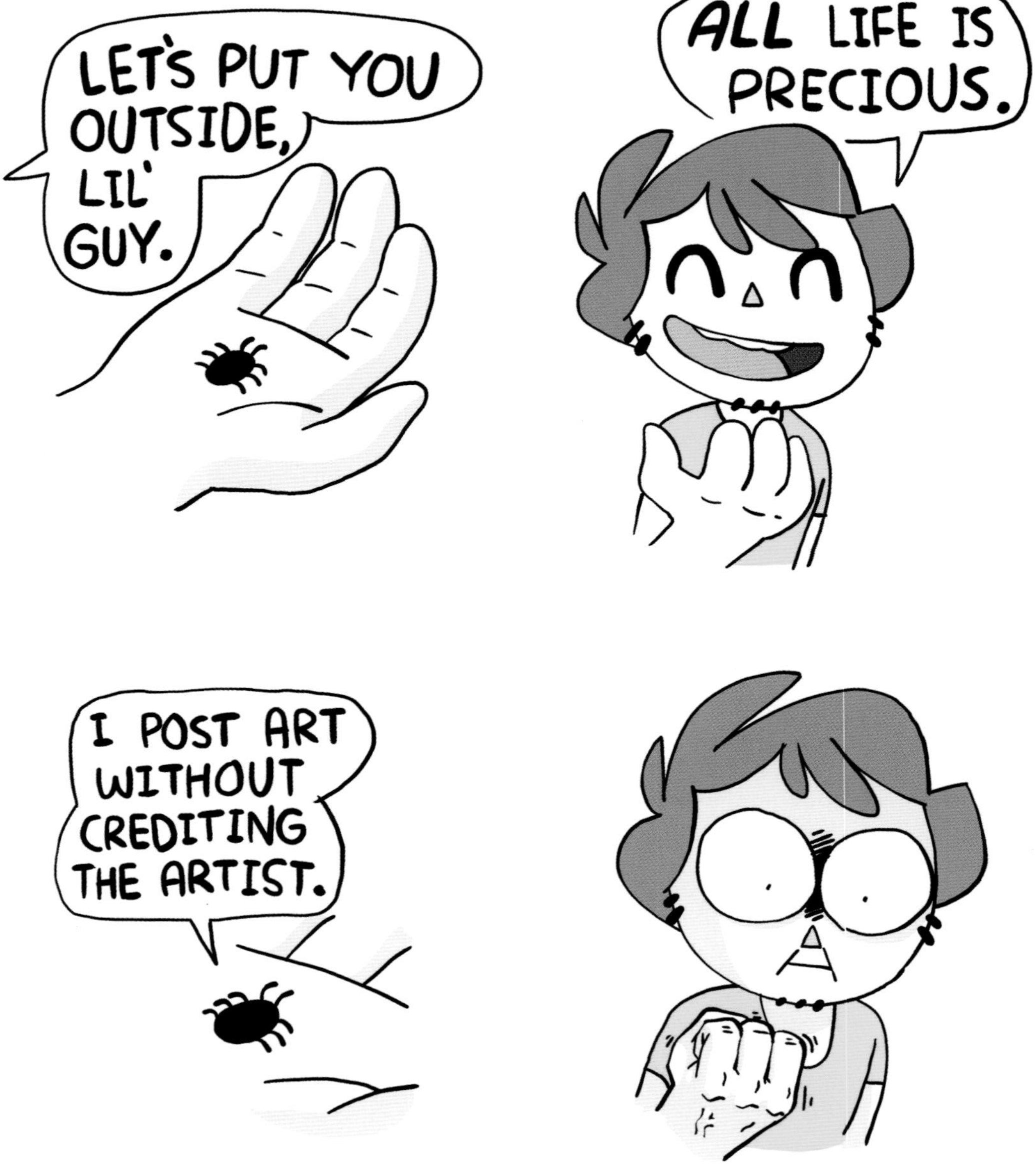
LET'S PUT YOU OUTSIDE, LIL' GUY.
ALL LIFE IS PRECIOUS.
I POST ART WITHOUT CREDITING THE ARTIST.

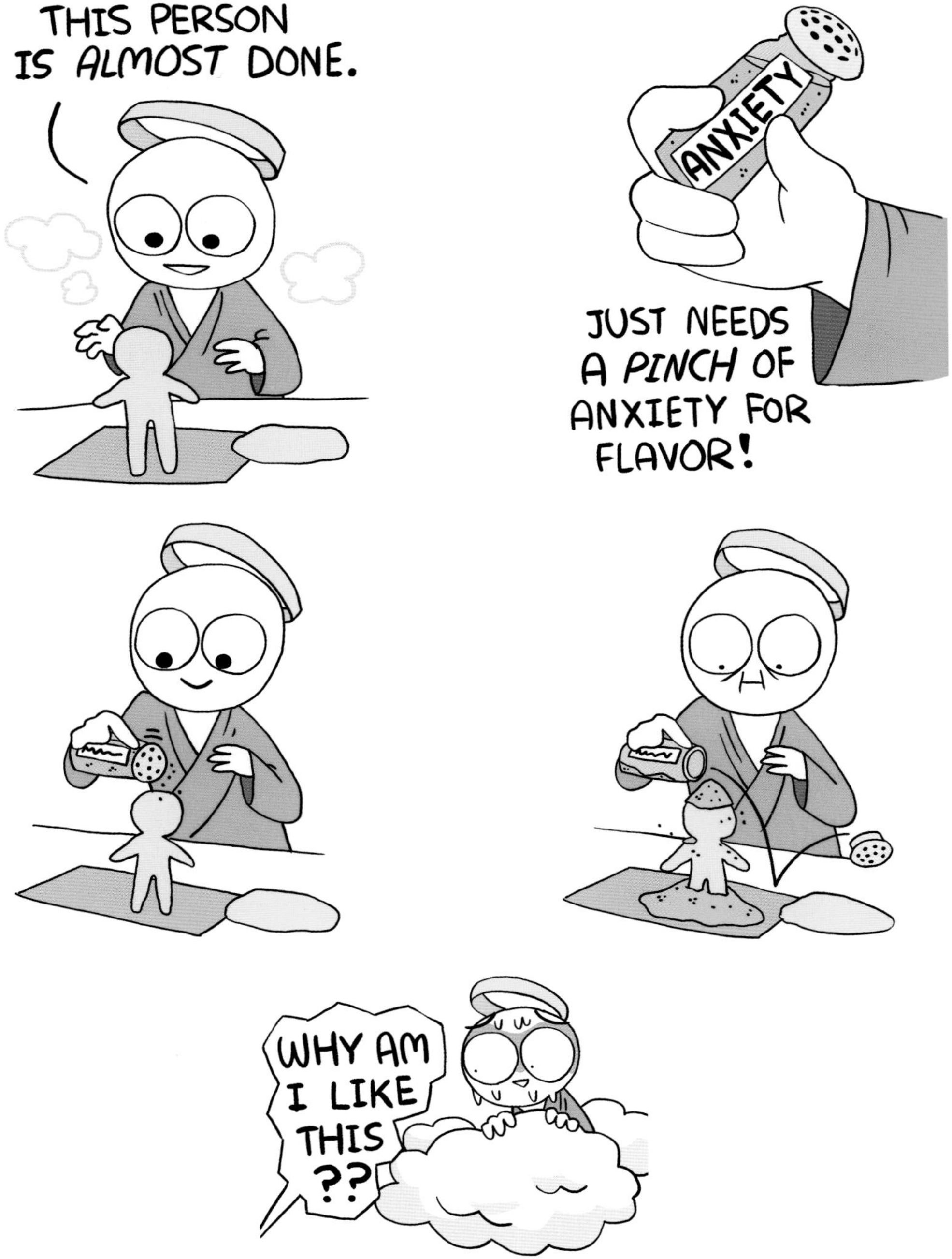
THIS PERSON IS ALMOST DONE.
ANXIETY
JUST NEEDS A PINCH OF ANXIETY FOR FLAVOR!
WHY AM I LIKE THIS ??

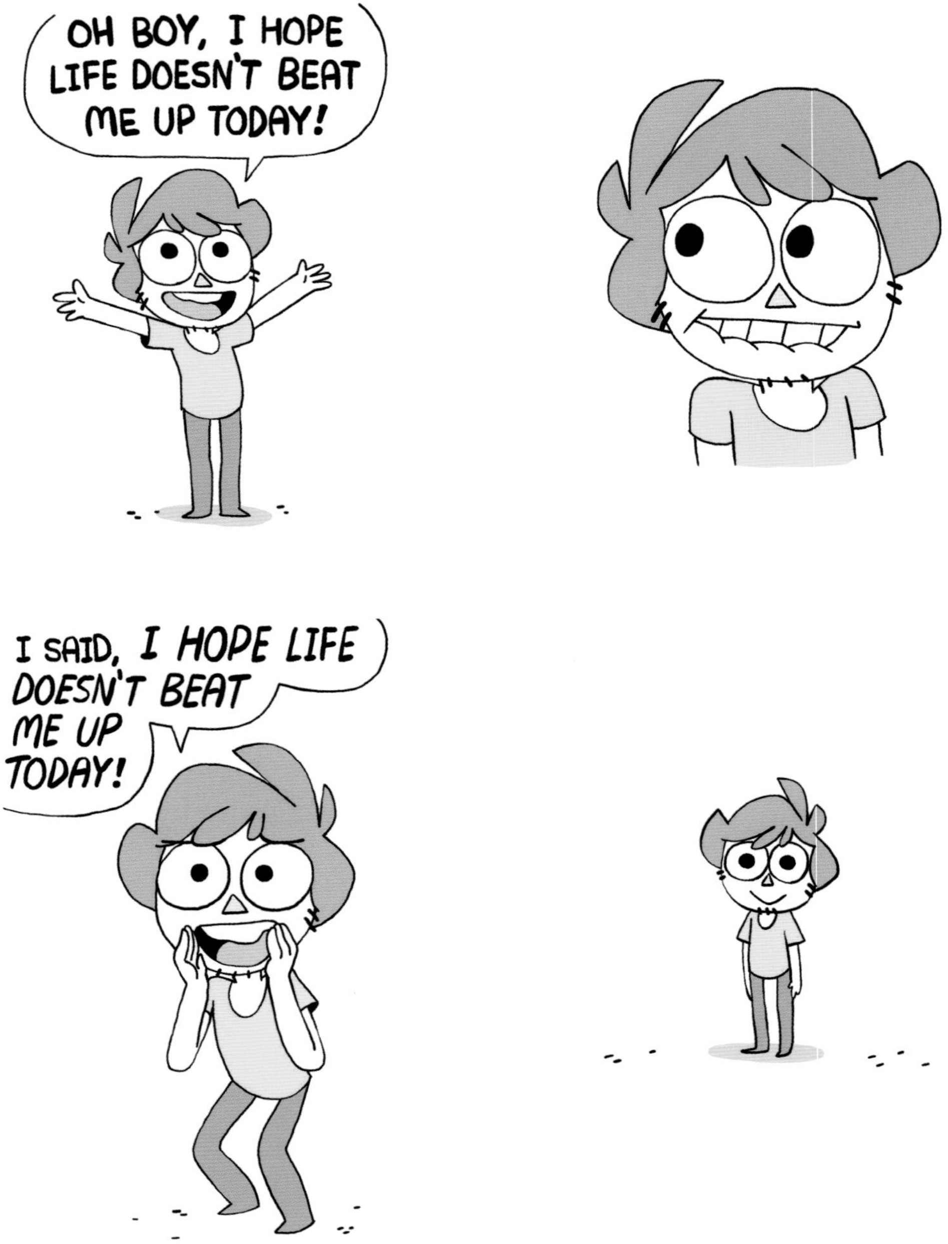
OH BOY, I HOPE LIFE DOESN'T BEAT ME UP TODAY!
I SAID, I HOPE LIFE DOESN'T BEAT ME UP TODAY!

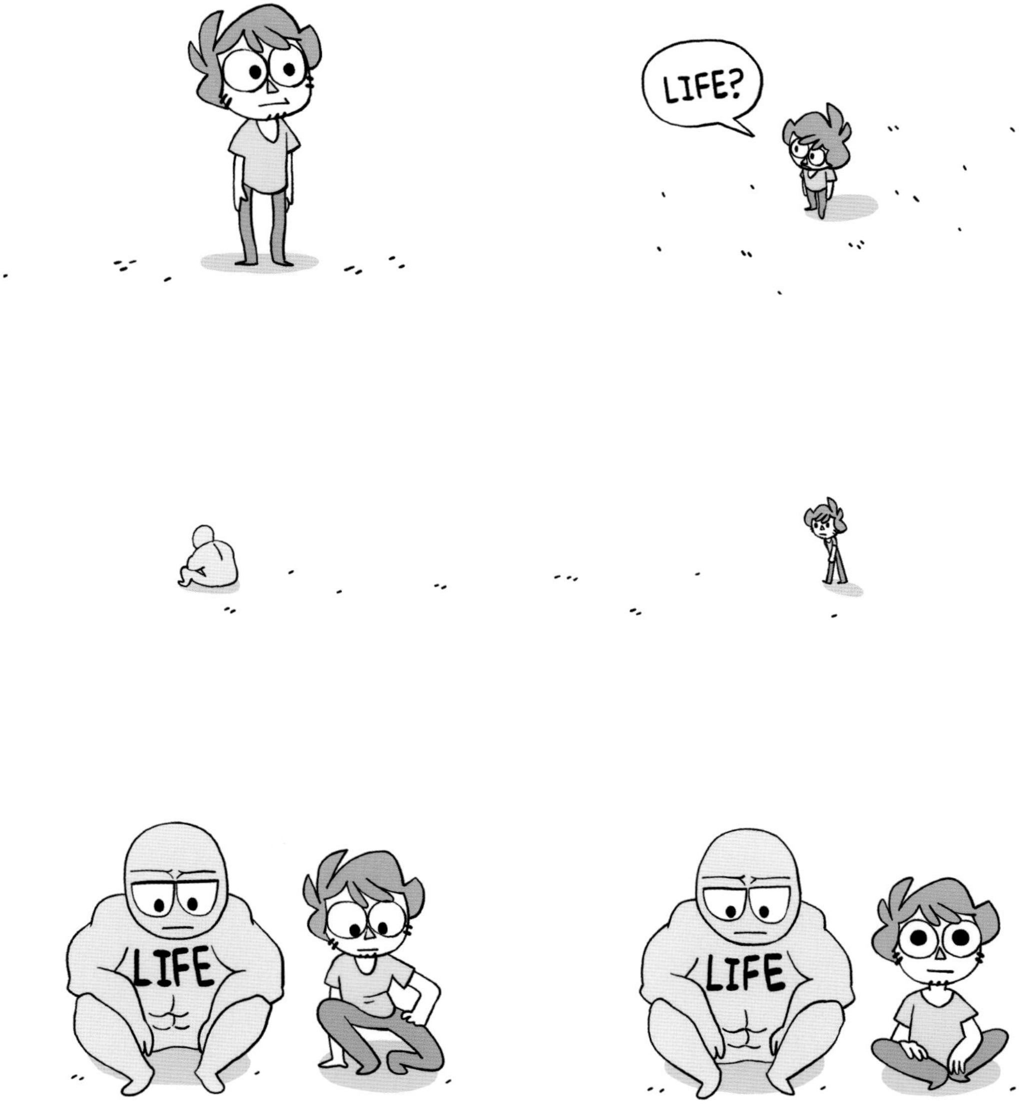
LIFE?
LIFE
LIFE

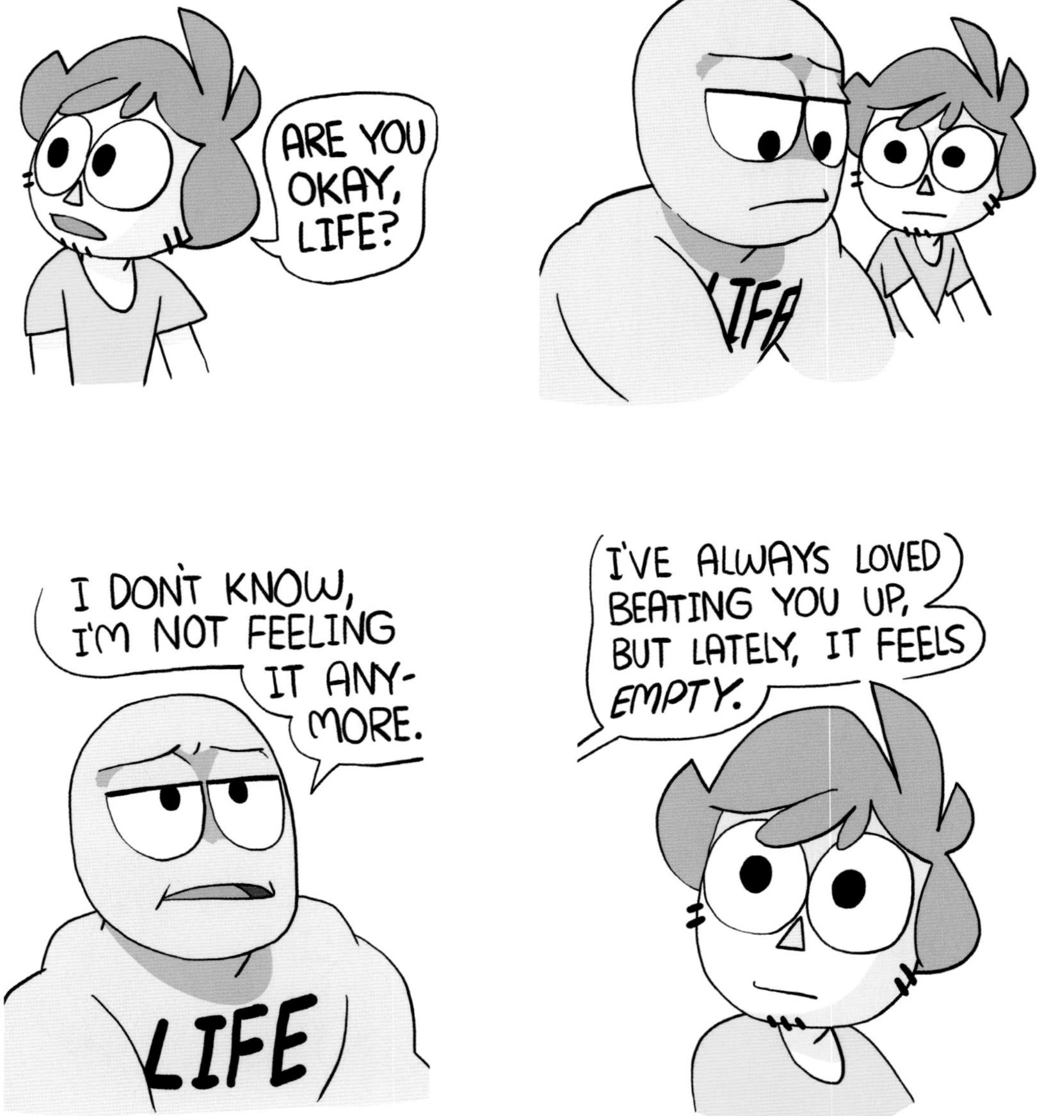
ARE YOU OKAY, LIFE?
LIFE
I DON'T KNOW, I'M NOT FEELING IT ANY-MORE.
LIFE
I'VE ALWAYS LOVED BEATING YOU UP, BUT LATELY, IT FEELS *EMPTY*.

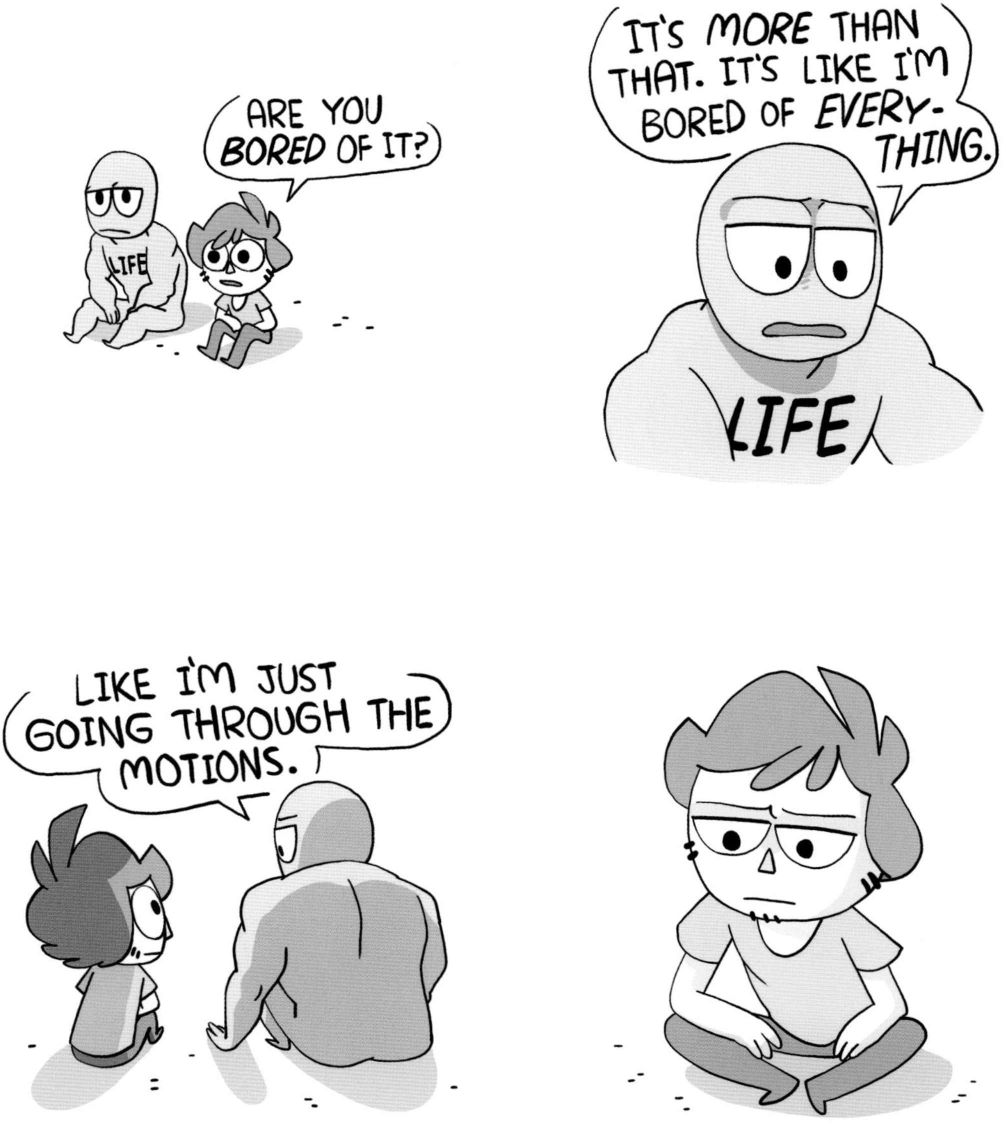
ARE YOU BORED OF IT?
LIFE
IT'S MORE THAN THAT. IT'S LIKE I'M BORED OF EVERY-THING.
LIFE
LIKE I'M JUST GOING THROUGH THE MOTIONS.

WELL, Y'KNOW.

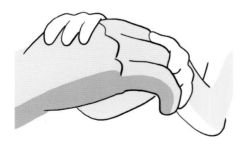

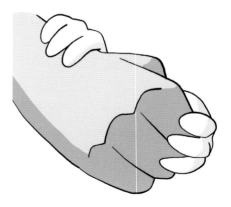

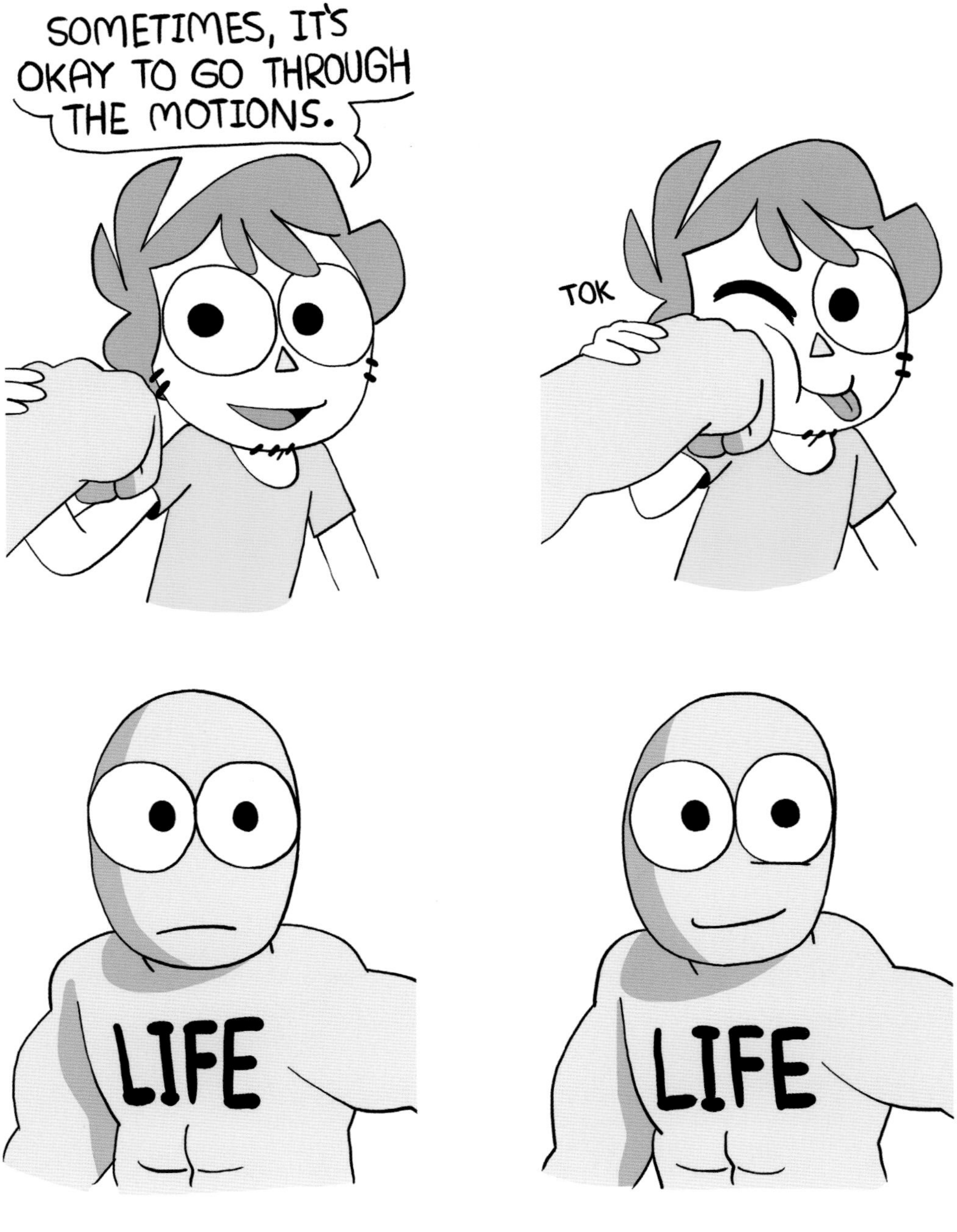
SOMETIMES, IT'S OKAY TO GO THROUGH THE MOTIONS.
TOK
LIFE
LIFE

THANK YOU
FOR READING!

Andrews McMeel Publishing
a division of Andrews McMeel Universal
1130 Walnut Street, Kansas City, Missouri 64106

18 19 20 21 22 SDB 10 9 8 7 6 5 4 3 2 1

ISBN: 978-1-4494-8693-8

Library of Congress Control Number: 2016957827

Editor: Lucas Wetzel
Art Director: Holly Swayne
Production Editor: Amy Strassner
Production Manager: Tamara Haus

www.andrewsmcmeel.com
www.shencomix.com

ATTENTION: SCHOOLS AND BUSINESSES
Andrews McMeel books are available at quantity discounts with bulk purchase for educational, business, or sales promotional use. For information, please e-mail the Andrews McMeel Publishing Special Sales Department: specialsales@amuniversal.com.